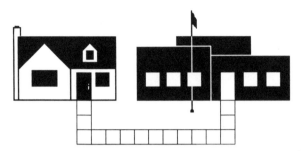

THE HOME & SCHOOL CONNECTION

How Your Home Life Affects Your Child's Success at School

Dr. T. Lee Burnham

SHADOW MOUNTAIN®

Salt Lake City, Utah

Shadow Mountain is an imprint of Deseret Book Company,
P.O. Box 30178, Salt Lake City, Utah 84130.

First printing August 1986

Library of Congress Cataloging-in-Publication Data

Burnham, T. Lee, 1942–
    The home and school connection.

    Includes index.
    1. Home and school—United States.   2. School
children—United States—Family relationships.
3. Community and school—United States.   I. Title.
LC225.3.B774 1986   370.19′3   86-15418
ISBN 0-87579-045-3 (pbk.)

*In loving memory of my wife, Judy Kay,
who recognized the need for early education
in the home and whose son will always
benefit from her loving teaching.*

*Also in memory of my father, who taught
me how to learn and to love learning.*

Contents

Preface

In bringing this book to the light of day, I must admit to feeling more like an editor than an author. This represents material that I have collected over the years as well as created to teach classes and help clients. Much of this material is not original with me, but perhaps the way it is organized and presented will make it useful to the reader.

I am convinced that parents can make the difference in their children's education. All that most parents require is the knowledge of what to do and why.

In expressing gratitude to those who assisted with this book, I find that I must begin with my parents. My mother was trained as a teacher. My father left formal schooling after the eighth grade but continued to learn and study on his own to gain an education that rivals anything I have been able to obtain through the formal educational system. I can never adequately thank either of them.

Merritt Egan, Virginia Frobes, Calvin Taylor, and Joe Bentley taught me the importance of human relationships and started me on the road that led to this book. Joe Bentley encouraged me to go to Minnesota, where the foundation of this book began.

The faculty of the University of Minnesota, Alan Anderson, Clyde Parker, Lynn Scoresby, Margaret Hoopes, David Johnson, Howard Williams, Theda Hagenah, Bill Edson, Bruce Sillers, and John Rhetts imbued me with a philosophy that made it necessary for me to be concerned about how to teach people in organizations to meet the needs of individuals.

Friends like Carole Widick, Lance Hurt, Mary Leonard, and

Mary Brabeck combined their thoughts and efforts to study what was happening to children in school and how we could teach teachers to do a better job. It was from their efforts that I came to look more closely at what impact parents could have on children's education.

Lynn Scoresby invited me to do my first workshop, entitled "Helping Children Succeed in School." This workshop and a series of others aimed at helping parents to be more effective produced the material contained in this volume.

How can I thank the hundreds of parents at PTA meetings and parenting workshops who made suggestions and listened patiently while I figured out what I really wanted to say.

My sisters made much of this book possible. Barbara helped me to find the right words to express my thoughts. Joan helped to take care of both me and my son. Evva Jean was always there, particularly during times of trauma that would have turned to utter panic without her.

Support and friendship from Ross and Marge Olsen during times of personal sorrow made continued work on this volume possible.

Understanding and careful editing by Jack Lyon put the finishing touches on this effort. He even persuaded me to change the original title (*Who Is Failing Whom?*) to the present one. And what would I have done if my faithful word processor had not decided to function flawlessly (finally) after ten months of regular monthly repairs.

And last but not least, I thank my son Clinton. Because he is so easy to get along with and makes being a father such a joy, this volume was completed.

Introduction

Contrary to popular mythology, our ability to learn increases with age rather than diminishes. Only death or senility can put a stop to that increase. Research and observation tell us, however, that many individuals over the age of twenty seem to have stopped learning. (There would seem, then, to be many dead or senile people wandering around out there.) We have done a beautiful job of teaching people that the only way to learn is in a classroom, and we have taught that even in a classroom people learn only if they have to. To get a grade. To get a diploma. To get a job. To keep their parents happy. How did we ever create such a situation?

In the past few years, parents have been asking just that. A great deal of criticism has been leveled at our schools, where test scores seem to indicate a steady decline in student performance. A few remedies have been tried, with little result.

Before a school even opens its doors, two major factors have already greatly determined what will happen in the classroom: first, the training and experience of the teachers, and second, the basic attitudes and learning skills that students bring from home. Of course, other problems exist in the schools themselves, but many of them are related to these two basic elements.

Teacher education programs make little if any real impact on how teachers actually function in the classroom. A report by the American Association of Colleges for Teacher Education speaks of "smugness where there should be concern" and complains that "the moderate and the mild control the destiny of education. They desire change but the change is only some modest tinkering." What seems clearly evident is that we have problems in our educational system and that these problems have left many people lacking in basic skills.

Teacher education programs seem to have a built-in bias toward those who are rigid in their approach to problems. Emphasis is given to organization and classroom control. What is wrong with teacher education, in short, is not just that too much time is devoted to "how-to" courses, but that these courses teach little more than how to bore students. More important than the actual content of courses is how the courses are taught. Example is a powerful tool for teaching. Most teachers have had many years to observe ineffective examples of teaching, leading, and parenting. Because we have a strong tendency to model our efforts after the examples we have seen, good or bad, we must create opportunities for prospective teachers to experience effective teaching.

Much is known about the knowledge and skills teachers need. But we seem unable to allow what we know about effective teaching skills to have much effect on the way we train and reward teachers. For example: Researchers have examined the skills and knowledge needed to deal with problems openly and creatively. Much of this research is on competition and cooperation and gives us valuable information about the need to develop a supportive and cooperative classroom atmosphere. Studies indicate that classrooms organized so that students cooperate with each other rather than compete produce the following results:

1. Discussions are friendlier.
2. Students learn each other's names more rapidly.
3. Students are more satisfied with discussions.
4. Students are more attentive to and more influenced by what is said in the classroom.
5. Students feel less anxiety.

In spite of evidence of the need to develop cooperation, teacher education programs make little effort to teach how that is done. In fact, most educators blindly insist on competition. Use of the normal curve in grading, for example, creates competition and meaningless grades. There is no justification for using it. The competition it produces is very destructive. Continued use of the normal curve instead of criterion-referenced grading can be excused only because most teachers simply do not know any better, do not know what else to do, or are forced by administrators to use it.

An important consideration in selecting and educating teachers is the personality characteristics and human relation skills that influence learning. A teacher's personality is very important, particularly with students who are insecure or who have poor opinions about school and themselves. How a teacher behaves, not what a teacher knows, may be the most important factor in how well students learn. A teacher's lack of sensitivity will markedly reduce students' self-esteem and ability to learn. Students of more empathic teachers improve significantly more in reading achievement than do students of less empathic teachers. Truancy rates are lower for students of teachers with high empathy. Even in college, students taught by teachers trained in interpersonal relations made greater gains than did their counterparts. Research indicates that student achievement is related to the interpersonal skills of the teacher.

Assuming that teachers have mastered their subjects, we should focus on training them in the kind of interpersonal relationships with students that will help them grow and learn. Both learning and development by the pupil and by the teacher can emerge from a process of interaction and cooperation. Even evaluation in the classroom needs to be based upon trust and openness rather than upon competition. Teachers should have the skills to create a safe learning climate where each student is accepted as a person with feelings that are not to be invalidated. A teacher's understanding of others and personal mannerisms can create a climate for growth and learning.

Many teachers seem unable to distinguish between the frustration that comes from grappling with difficult intellectual material and the frustration from lack of student-teacher rapport. Teachers can be more effective in the classroom if they can identify emotions of students and communicate effectively with them. Warmth, empathy, and genuineness are vital if learning and personal growth are to take place.

Too often we see people who have become administrators and counselors because they were not successful in the classroom and have come to dislike students. This dislike will often arise out of personal and professional frustration resulting from ineffective interpersonal and problem-solving skills. Such people are usually rigid and unable to relate to the needs of young people. As a result, we see school systems run by those mainly concerned with rules and procedures when what we need are school systems run by caring, creative individuals, who are, of course, intellectually competent. Today, we risk causing great harm to a large number of our youth. We need to spend more time creating an environment that will entice students to want to learn rather than trying to control students as we attempt to force them to learn.

Our first major problem, then, is that we have failed to adequately prepare people to be effective teachers. We can be thankful that many teachers are effective in the classroom because of the kind of people they are and the kinds of examples they have observed in their own school experience, but not because of their training. Many other teachers should never have become teachers. Their personality, their motives, and their approach to students make it impossible for them ever to become effective teachers, even with the most powerful training. Still another group of teachers could have be effective if their training had not failed to give them the tools they need to succeed. Many of these teachers become frustrated and either leave the field of education or continue to struggle, taking many of their students with them as they sink into the mire of self-doubt, apathy, and failure. If we are going to solve the problems in our schools, we must greatly overhaul our inadequate attempts at teacher education.

Our second major problem, and the main focus of this book, has to do with the attitudes and skills that students bring to school from home. Some recent writers have been quite forceful in their contention that our present educational problems are entirely the fault of the public school system and a certain approach or a certain amount of money will solve these problems. This tends to focus the attention of committees and legislatures on quick-fix remedies that address neither teacher selection and training nor home-inspired student attitudes and skills. Thus, these two vital areas continue to be overlooked and unimproved.

In spite of all of the problems with poorly trained teachers and rigid administrators, many students still succeed. There are three groups of students in most schools. One group comes from homes that are so supportive of the learning process and so good at teaching basic learning skills that the students will do well no matter what kind of learning environment they encounter. A second group comes from homes that are so negative that there is nothing the best teachers or the most effective schools can do to help them. The third and perhaps largest group comes from homes and families that are just there. They have little effect on how well their children do in school. These students will probably do well in school if the teachers in their early grades have personalities that they can relate to and if the relationships they build with other students are satisfying. When these two conditions exist, the students gain a positive attitude toward school that lasts as long as parental and peer influence remain positive.

Some children do seem to refuse to respond to their environment. Even if their family provides them with every opportunity and skill, they may choose to ignore all of that and fail at everything, including school. Others seem to manage to succeed and to achieve in spite of all the roadblocks that have been placed in their way. Most children, however, respond to the environment that they are placed in and act accordingly.

Several years ago a research project was carried out with three hundred children who had been identified by their teachers as having behavior problems. One-third of these students were placed in a special program where they received counseling, tutoring, and anything else that they might need to help them. Another third had the same type of program with special attention and training for the parents and the teachers. The last group was left completely alone; all of the attention was focused on the parents and the teachers. Only students in the last group showed significant improvement. Does that tell us something about how to affect students? Improve the environment, and you will see progress in the student!

Children learn or fail to learn essential skills and attitudes about learning, school, and teachers during the first five years of their lives. With the powerful influences from television and other outside forces, parents must be more aware of what they can do to develop a positive influence in the home; otherwise they invite trouble. Because many parents lack this awareness, many children do not learn the skills they need and may even learn attitudes and skills that make success in school difficult or impossible. But parents can significantly affect the success of their children at school. This book tells how.

1

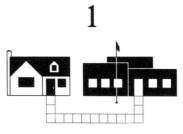

Communication in the Home

Several years ago, a child was labeled by teachers and counselors as having a severe learning disability with possible organic brain damage. A complete evaluation, however, indicated no sign of any organic problem, but the child had not learned to think or communicate well. Further investigation revealed that this youngster was almost never given the opportunity to talk. His parents did not talk much, and they listened to him not at all. The communication in their home was limited to brief commands and put-downs: "Don't do that!" "Not now!" "Go away!" "Why are you so dumb?" As a result, the child did not learn how to talk, think, or listen.

After counseling, this family began to change their communication patterns, and the child began to talk more and learn. Now he is working at an appropriate grade-level and is doing quite well.

When children hear only short sentences at home, they will find it difficult or impossible to listen to teachers who speak in whole paragraphs. The teachers may wonder why their instructions are never understood, but in fact they are not even being heard.

A group of parents in a parenting class were assigned to tape-record their interactions with their children for one week. On one of the tapes, a five-year-old said, "Guess what, Mommy. I learned today that butterflies come from green frogs." The mother later said that she was just about to reply, "What a silly thing to say!" when she remembered that she was being taped, and that her instructor would scold her if she said that. So the mother got down on the floor so that she would be at the child's level and said, "That's interesting; tell me more about that." The child replied, "I was only teasing, Mommy." Then the child began a long dialogue about several things that were on her mind. She was not going to share anything important with her mother until she knew that her mother was going to listen.

Children often test parents that way. Teenagers often say something that seems way out in left field to see if we are going to listen or if we are going to overreact, evaluate, or reply with sarcasm. Children need to learn to think. They will not learn to do that very well unless they have opportunities to talk, to express their ideas. To do that they must have adults around them who will listen to them. When children are unsure of an adult's willingness to listen, they will test the adult with meaningless or even objectionable talk. If the adult sticks with them for a few minutes, they will stop testing and begin to share what they are really thinking. They will not share their feelings unless they know they can do so without criticism.

If you want to communicate effectively with your children, follow these guidelines: (1) Make sure that you are on the same level as your children (eye to eye). Do not hover over them. (2) Make a statement or ask a question that will indicate your readiness to listen. Use open statements or questions that invite a lengthy reply instead of a simple yes or no.

Teenagers listen to their parents about a thousandth as much as they feel their parents listen to them. So if you want your teenagers to listen to you, listen to them a lot as they grow up. This listening will also help your children do better in school.

I asked a group of students to think about the communication patterns in their homes. They were to write down what they felt were the unwritten rules. One of the most common rules was: "No one in this family has a right to express a thought or a feeling without being made fun of, criticized, or evaluated." Often father or mother were exempt from this rule, but seldom if ever were both exempt, and even less often were any of the children exempt from it. Such an environment teaches children to keep their thoughts and feelings to themselves, or to say or feel only what is expected of them. In both cases a child's ability to learn is severly hindered if not destroyed.

Children need to know that their parents are not going to say to the neighbors, "You know what my crazy kid said yesterday?" Preserve the confidence of the things your children tell you. Don't spread them all over, even if you think that they are "cute." If you feel you must share something, first ask the child's permission.

If your child says something that disturbs you, do not react strongly at the time. Remain calm and think about it for a day or two. If it still bothers you and you think that it is something that needs correcting, find a quiet moment when you both feel good about each other and say, "Remember the other day when we were talking, and you said ———. Well, I have been thinking about that, and I would like to share with you how I feel about that." Then share your feelings and thoughts. Remember that your intention is to share how you feel and what you think. Do not try to convince or lecture. When you think you have expressed yourself adequately, ask for your child's feelings and wait for a response. In most instances, children will consider and usually adopt your point of view as long as it is reasonable and is presented as your point of view rather than as an ultimatum.

Encourage your children to write down what they think and feel. Keeping journals is a great idea for teenagers. It will help them get their thoughts and feelings outside themselves where they can be examined. Many small things that seem overly important begin to be seen in proper perspective when they are written down.

Poor communication is a crucial problem in family life. We often hear about a "lack of communication." Many assume that verbal communication is the most important kind. But perhaps most problems come from poor nonverbal communication. The person who says little but greets every communication from children with sighs, groans, shrugs, or apathy may do much more damage to a relationship than one who explodes.

Failure to recognize and allow for personality differences also causes problems. To expect the same type of communication from an introvert as from an extrovert is simply not realistic. Sometimes children do not talk about the thoughts and feelings that are important to them because they have found that their style of communicating is not accepted by other members of their family. So they learn to play a certain role and to hide their true thoughts and feelings.

Communication difficulties generally arise in four areas:

1. The expression of thoughts and ideas.

2. The ability to listen and correctly interpret what others are trying to say.

3. Nonverbal expressions of which the communicator is completely unaware.

4. The ability to allow for and accept individual differences.

Although communication is often defined as talking, the ability to listen is perhaps a more important part of communication for parents. Parents who do not listen are teaching their children not to talk. Parents can become better listeners by following these guidelines:

1. Don't interrupt.

2. Don't argue.

3. Encourage your children to talk by giving them your full attention, nods of approval or understanding, and obvious interest.

4. Recognize the advantage of letting your children blow off steam. If you look interested and pay full attention, they will be satisfied. Children are usually more interested in being listened to than they are in receiving advice or solving problems.

5. As a good listener, you do not have to agree with your children. Your responsibility is to listen and to let them know that you are listening. You need to let them know that you understand what they are trying to say, but you do not need to agree with them.

Listening is tied to loving. If you really love others, you will have genuine concern for what they have to say. Listening is much more than the mechanical act of hearing. Listening is giving close attention in order to gain information and show understanding. One of the great skills of communication is the ability to listen with understanding. Many of us feel we are good listeners just because we have the self-restraint to be quiet while another is talking. However, there is a big difference between just sitting there, and actively listening with understanding. To listen with understanding is to share with speakers their perceptions and emotions. It is to "walk for a while in their moccasins." Listening is active. A good listener is involved, interested, concerned.

James Stephens wrote, "I have learned that the head does not hear anything until the heart has listened, and that what the heart knows today the head will understand tomorrow." Listen with the heart. Practice empathy. Put yourself in your children's place and try to hear their problems in your heart.

Listen with patience. Your children deserve unhurried time. Even five minutes can be made unhurried if your attitude is right. Listen with compassion and with depth. Create a climate in which your children may confidently speak, an atmosphere of candor, consideration, and kindness that permits and encourages your children to say those significant words, "I need help." Listen to help and to comfort.

Students of various ages were asked, "How do you tell if a teacher is really listening to you?" Some significant things can be learned from their answers. A seventy-one-year-old woman said, "He asks me questions about what I am saying, so that I feel free to tell him some more. He can repeat what I have said, so I know he listened to me." Some comments from ten- and eleven-year-old boys were: "She turns around and looks at me." "She acts like she has time to stop." "Her face looks interested." A forty-six-year-old man said, "He understands how I am feeling at the moment. He says things that make me know he is trying to understand what I am feeling as well as what I am saying." A class of seventeen-year-old and eighteen-year-old girls made these comments: "She doesn't interrupt me." "She pays full attention to me. I can tell by her eyes and what she says to me." "She doesn't start giving advice before I even get finished with what I am saying."

What conclusions can be drawn from these statements? An active listener facilitates communication through:

1. Interested facial expression.
2. Appropriate, thoughtful questions and comments about what is being said.
3. Calm, alert attitude.
4. Eye-to-eye contact.

A disinterested, inactive listener inhibits communication by:

1. Fidgeting, looking nervous, or being anxious to cut off the conversation.
2. Interrupting frequently.
3. Ignoring the feeling behind the words.
4. Giving unasked-for advice and judgments.
5. Giving a "blank look."
6. Making comments that are irrelevant to the conversation.
7. Looking away.

A parent who fails to listen is likely to be as ineffective as a doctor who does not listen to a description of symptoms and cannot accurately understand or diagnose the underlying disease. Parents cannot effectively help their children when they do not understand their children's questions, problems, and conflicts. Understanding parents listen to a child and watch for clues in posture, facial expressions, and tone of voice. They do not jump to conclusions about the child, giving advice or preaching about what the child should do when all the child really wants is a listening ear.

Research has shown that about 70 percent of our communication with others is carried out nonverbally. How people stand, hold their heads, drum their fingers, smile, or frown are important and say much more than words. Usually, however, we perceive these messages inaccurately and subconsciously and find ourselves in big trouble with little or no awareness of the interaction taking place. Every action provides a sensory cue that can be read in one way or another.

Those who are acutely aware of these cues and responses are often able to add up the sensory data and then jump beyond them to another level of understanding. This can be helpful with children, because we may be able to understand what is bothering them before they even begin to speak to us. Parents with this ability can guide their children in their attempts to express what is going on inside them. Misread a nonverbal cue, however, and you may try to force your children into a feeling that they do not really have. When you are making assumptions based on nonverbal cues, you have to treat your assumptions as tentative. Paraphrase to find out if your perceptions are accurate, and make sure that people do not get the feeling that you are trying to force them into meeting your assumptions or expectations. Don't force people into corners.

By being sensitively aware of nonverbal clues, we can learn when to avoid the wrong moment to begin speaking and how to untangle confusions caused by confusing messages. A father may say to a child, "I'm listening, I'm listening," while his eyes are glued to the television set. The child may not understand why he feels so confused and unable to say anything. One message says "I'm listening" while another message says "Can't you see I'm busy? Go away."

Children with parents to whom they can confidently and comfortably talk and who will listen to them are fortunate. Many children have parents who seem uninterested in anything children have to say. It may seem that the parents do not want to be part of any meaningful communication, but perhaps it is just that they do not know how.

Responses that parents typically make to children's messages are, in many circumstances, perfectly appropriate. But there are some responses that can build barriers and cut off further expression from the child. Some of these are:

1. *Directing, ordering, commanding ("You must . . . ," "You have to . . . ," "You will . . . ").* Such responses can produce fear or even resistance and rebellion. They also invite "testing." Nobody likes to be ordered or commanded. Such responses may cut off any further communication from the child, or they may provoke defensive or retaliatory commu-

nication. Often children will feel rejected — their needs are being ignored. In front of others, children may feel humiliated by such responses. Even if children obey, they may try to get back at the adult later, or they may respond immediately with anger.

2. *Warning, threatening, admonishing ("You had better . . . ," "If you don't, then . . . ")*. Such responses are like directing or ordering, except that the adult brings in the threat of using power. These responses invite "testing." They may cause the child to obey but only out of fear. As with directing and ordering, these responses may produce resentment, anger, resistance, and rebellion.

3. *Moralizing, preaching, obliging ("You should . . . ," "You ought to . . . ," "It is your duty to . . . ," "It is your responsibility . . . ," "You are required . . . ")*. Such responses are like directing and ordering except that the adults are dragging in "duty" and some vague external authority. Their purpose is to make the child feel guilty or to feel an obligation. Children sense the pressure of such messages and frequently resist them. Such messages also communicate lack of trust: "You are not wise enough." Children often respond with, "Who says I should?" or "Why should I?"

4. *Persuading with logic, arguing, instructing, lecturing ("Do you realize . . . ," "Here is why you are wrong . . . ," "That is not right . . . ," "The facts are . . . ," "Yes, but . . . ")*. Such responses provoke defensiveness and often bring counterarguments. They may also make children feel inferior because they imply the adult's superiority. Persuasion, more often than not, simply makes children defend their own position more strongly. Children may say, "You think you are always right." Having logic on your side does not always bring compliance or agreement. Children often say, "I always get long lectures," or "My parents make me feel I'm wrong or stupid."

5. *Advising, recommending, providing answers or solutions ("What I would do is . . . ," "Why don't you . . . ," "Let me suggest . . . ," "It would be best for you . . . ")*. It is not true that people always want advice. Advice implies superi-

ority and can make children feel inadequate and inferior: "I should have thought of that." Children may respond to such advice with resistance and rebellion: "I don't want to be told what to do." Often children resent suggestions from adults: "Let me figure it out myself." Failure to follow an adult's advice may make children feel guilty or that they have let the adult down. Advice can also make children dependent; it does not encourage their own creative thinking. A child may simply respond by feeling that the adult just doesn't understand. Also, if the adult's advice turns out wrong, the child can duck responsibility: "He suggested it; it wasn't my idea."

6. *Evaluating, condemning, disapproving, blaming, name-calling, criticizing ("You are bad"; "You are lazy"; "You are not thinking straight"; "You are acting foolishly.").* More than any other type of message, this makes children feel inferior, incompetent, bad, or stupid. It can make them feel guilty, too. Often children respond very defensively—nobody likes to be wrong. Evaluation cuts off communication: "I won't tell them what I feel if I am going to be judged." Because adults are authority figures, children often accept such judgments as being absolutely true: "I am bad." Evaluation by adults shapes children's self-concepts: "I am a slow learner"; "I am not pretty." Another response of children to evaluation by adults is to evaluate right back: "You're not so good yourself." Remember the adage "Judge not, lest ye be judged."

7. *Praising, evaluating positively, approving ("You're a good boy"; "You've done a good job"; "That's a very good drawing"; "That's a nice thing to do.").* Praise and positive evaluation may not always have the effect we would like. Sometimes children feel that praise is manipulative or simply false. Praise at an inappropriate moment can stop communication from children. There are times when any evaluation or judgment, even positive, can embarrass children or even make them angry. A child may think the adult is trying to look superior. What the child may really need is a nonevaluative listener. In some situations, children cannot separate praise from expectation. Thus, what is meant as reward comes across as implied

threat: "I will continue to be pleased with you as long as you continue to please me."

8. *Supporting, reassuring, excusing, sympathizing ("It's not so bad . . . ," "Don't worry," "You'll feel better . . . ," "That's too bad . . .").* Adults often try to reassure children without understanding the negative effect they are having. To reassure children may make them feel that you don't understand them. They may think: "It is easy for you to say that, but you don't know how I feel." Supporting messages can also convey to the child this meaning: "I'm not comfortable having you feel inadequate. I can't accept such feelings; start feeling more adequate." If things do not "turn out all right" for a child, then he can feel resentful toward you for your reassurance, for misleading him. Telling a child who feels unattractive to girls that he is really quite good-looking can evoke strong feelings of hostility. He may say in disbelief, "You're just saying that to make me feel better." Typical responses of children are these: "But Mother, I am ugly." "I don't want another boyfriend, I want him." "You don't understand — I'll always be dumb in math."

9. *Diagnosing, psychoanalyzing, interpreting ("What you need is . . . ," "What's wrong with you is . . . ," "You're just trying to get attention"; "You don't really mean that"; "I know what you need"; "Your real problem is . . .").* To tell children what they are "really" feeling, what their "real" motives are, or why they behave the way they do can be very threatening. They may think, "My parents always think they know what I'm feeling." Playing psychoanalyst with children is dangerous and frustrating to them. If your analysis is wrong, they resist it; if it is right, they may feel exposed, naked, trapped. The "here-is-what-you-need" message implies that the parents are superior — that they know more than the child. Children become resentful and angry when adults interpret their motives. Interpretations will usually stop communication from children rather than encourage them to tell you more.

10. *Questioning, probing, cross-examining, prying, interrogating ("Why . . . ?" "Who . . . ?" "Where . . . ?" "What . . . ?" "How . . . ?" "When . . . ?").* The response of children to

probing, like that of adults, is often to feel defensive or "on the witness stand." Many questions are threatening because the children don't know why their parents are questioning them. They may think, "What are you driving at?" Children often feel that adults are nosey. They may think, "She always has to know where I've been." Questioning can convey lack of trust, suspicion, or doubt about the child's ability, eliciting a response like, " You don't need to ask me if I know the way — I've been there before." Some kinds of probing questions make a child feel he is being led out on a limb only to have it sawed off later. ("When did you call Jane for the date? Only yesterday! Well, no wonder she already had a date.") When adults ask questions, they imply that they are gathering information so that they can solve their children's problems rather than let the children solve their problems themselves. A child may think, "If I tell my parents what they ask, then I have to listen to their answers." Questions drastically restrict the range of what children might say if they are allowed to speak spontaneously.

11. *Diverting, avoiding, bypassing, digressing, shifting ("Let's not talk about it now"; "Not at the dinner table"; "Forget it"; "That reminds me . . . "; "We can discuss it later.").* Such responses make children feel that parents are not interested. They may feel that their parents don't want to understand. These responses communicate a lack of respect and may make a child feel rejected or guilty.

12. *Kidding, teasing, making light of, joking, using sarcasm ("Why don't you burn down the school?" "When did you read a newspaper last?" "Get up on the wrong side of the bed?" "When did they make you principal of the school?").* Such responses effectively cut off communication, make children feel that parents are not interested, and show lack of respect. Or children may feel that parents really don't understand how badly or seriously they feel about something. Responses such as these often stem from hostility in the adult; consequently, they may provoke hostility in the child.

This is not to say that adults should never use any of these responses. It is to say that they should be more careful about these responses and try to encourage children to talk more instead of shutting them off.

If you tell somebody your phone number, he will usually repeat it to make sure he heard it correctly. However, if you make a complicated statement, most people will agree or disagree without trying to make sure that they are responding to what you really meant. Adults particularly seem to assume that what they understand from a child's statement is what the child really meant to say.

How do you check to make sure that you understand other people's ideas as they meant them? How do you know that what they say means the same thing to you as it does to them?

Of course, you can get children to clarify their remarks by asking, "What do you mean?" or "Tell me more" or by saying, "I don't understand." However, after they have elaborated, you still face the same question: "Am I understanding the idea as the child intends it to be understood?" Your feeling of certainty is no evidence that you do in fact understand.

If you state in your own way what your children's remarks mean to you, they can begin to determine whether their message is coming through as they intended. Then if they think you misunderstand, they can correct you. Paraphrasing is a way of revealing your understanding of another person's words to test your understanding. It is a way of being an active listener. An additional benefit of paraphrasing is that it lets others know that you are interested in them. It shows that you do want to understand what they mean. Then, they will probably be more willing to try to understand your views.

Paraphrasing is an important tool for clarifying understanding between adults and children. It increases the accuracy of communication and thus the degree of shared understanding. Paraphrasing conveys feelings — your interest in others, your concern to see how they view things.

Some might think of paraphrasing as merely putting someone's ideas in another way. They try to say the same thing with different words. Such word-swapping may result merely in the illusion of understanding. For example:

Sarah: Jim should never have become a teacher.

Fred: You mean teaching isn't the right job for Jim?

Sarah: Exactly! Teaching is not the right job for Jim.

Instead of trying to reword Sarah's statement, Fred might have asked himself, "What does Sarah's statement mean to me?" In that case, the interchange might have sounded like this:

Sarah: Jim should never have become a teacher.

Fred: You mean he is too harsh on the children?

Sarah: Oh, no. I meant that he has such expensive tastes that he can't ever earn enough as a teacher.

Fred: Oh, I see. You think he should have gone into a field that would have insured him a higher standard of living?

Sarah: Exactly! Teaching is not the right job for Jim.

Effective paraphrasing is not a trick or a verbal gimmick, although when you first try to use this skill, you will feel uncomfortable and unsure of yourself. Just give yourself some time. Effective paraphrasing requires a certain attitude that comes from a desire to know what the other person really means. To satisfy that desire, you share with that person the meaning his comment had for you so that he can check whether it matches the meaning he intended to convey.

If the other's statement was general, it may convey something specific to you:

Larry: I think this is a very poor textbook.

You: Poor? You mean it has too many inaccuracies?

Larry: No, the text is accurate, but the book comes apart too easily.

Possibly the other person's comment suggests an example to you:

Laura: This text has too many omissions; we shouldn't adopt it.

You: You mean that the book does not cover all time periods in American history equally well?

Laura: Yes, that's one example. It also lacks any discussion of the development of the arts in America.

If the speaker's comment was very specific, it may convey a more general idea to you:

Ralph: Do you have twenty-five pencils I can borrow for my class?

You: Do you just want something for them to write with? I have about fifteen ball-point pens and ten or eleven pencils.

Ralph: Great. Anything that writes will do.

Sometimes the other person's idea will suggest its inverse or opposite to you:

Stanley: I think the teacher's union acts so irresponsible because the administration has ignored them so long.

You: Do you mean the teacher's union would be less militant now if the administration had consulted with them in the past?

Another element important to clear communication is the expression of feelings. To communicate your own feelings accurately or to understand those of others is difficult. Expressions of emotion may take many forms. Feelings can express themselves in bodily changes, in actions, and in words. Any specific expression of feelings may actually express a variety of different feelings. A blush, for example, may indicate that someone is feeling pleased, but it may also indicate that the person feels annoyed, embarrassed, or uneasy. Likewise, a specific feeling is not always expressed in the same way. For example, a child's affection for his teacher may lead him to blush when she stands near his desk, to touch her as she passes, to watch her as she walks around the room, to tell her "You're nice," or to bring his pet turtle to show her. Different forms of expression indicate the child's affection.

When you are trying to understand someone's feelings, your perceptions are likely to be inaccurate and misleading. What you interpret as an expression of anger, for example, may instead mean hurt feelings or fear.

A further obstacle to understanding someone's feelings is that your perception of what he is feeling is based on so many different kinds of information. When somebody speaks, you notice more than just the words. You notice gestures, voice tone, posture, facial expression, and so on. In addition, you are aware of the immediate situation, the context in which the person is speaking. You are aware of whether someone else is listening, for example. So you make assumptions about how the situation influences what the other person is feeling. Also, you have expectations based on your past experiences with the person.

You make inferences from all of this information: words, nonverbal clues, the situation, your expectations. These inferences are influenced by how you feel at the time. What you perceive the person to be feeling, then, often depends more upon what you are feeling than upon the other person's actions or words. For example, if you are feeling guilty about something, you may perceive others as angry with you. If you are feeling depressed and discouraged, others may seem to be expressing disapproval of you.

Accurately communicating and understanding feelings is extremely difficult. Yet if you wish others to respond to you, you must help them understand how you feel. Likewise, if you are concerned about others, you must try to understand their feelings.

Although we usually try to describe our *ideas* clearly, we often do not try to describe our *feelings* clearly. One way to describe a feeling is to name it: "I feel embarrassed"; "I feel angry"; "I feel comfortable with you." However, we do not have enough names or labels to cover the broad range of human emotions, and so we invent other ways to describe our feelings, such as by using similes: "I feel like a small frog in a huge pond." A girl whose friendly overture had just been rebuffed said, "I feel like I just had an arm amputated."

A third way to describe a feeling is to report what kind of action the feeling urges you to take: "I feel like hugging and hugging you"; "I'd like to slap you"; "I wish I could walk off and leave you."

In addition, many figures of speech serve as descriptions of feelings: "I Just swallowed a bushel of spring sunshine."

When describing your feelings, try to make clear what they are. You can do this by using the words *I*, *me*, or *my* and by describing your feelings in words.

The following examples show the relation between two kinds of expressions of feeling, those that describe the emotional state and those that do not. Notice that expressions of feeling that describe the speaker's emotional state are more precise and less capable of misinterpretation.

Exressing feelings by describing the emotional state:	*Expressing feelings without describing the emotional state:*
"I feel embarrassed." "I feel pleased." "I feel annoyed."	Blushing and saying nothing.
"I feel angry." "I'm worried about this." "I feel hurt by what you said."	Suddenly becoming silent in the midst of a conversation.
"I enjoy her sense of humor." "I respect her abilities and competence." "I love her but I feel I shouldn't say so."	"She's a wonderful person."
"I hurt too much to hear any more." "I feel angry at myself." "I'm angry with you."	"Shut up!"

Describing your feelings should not be an effort to coerce the other person into changing so that you won't feel as you do. Rather, you report your inner state as one more piece of information that is necessary if the two of you are to understand and improve your relationship.

You might describe what you perceive to be the other person's inner state in order to check whether you understand what he feels. You transform his *expressions* of his feelings into a tentative *description* of his feelings. A good perception check conveys the message "I want to understand your feelings — is this the way you feel?" Here are some examples:

"I get the impression you are angry with me. Are you?" (*Not* : "Why are you so angry with me?" This is mind reading, not perception checking.)

"Am I right that you feel disappointed that nobody commented on your suggestion?"

"I'm not sure whether your expression means that my comment hurt your feelings, irritated you, or confused you."

Note that a perception check describes the other person's feelings and does not express disapproval or approval.

Learning to communicate well with others takes consistent effort. It may seem overwhelming at first, but you can start simply by trying to be a better listener. As you spend time listening, you will find that you have time to understand, to explore feelings, and to get closer to those around you. You will also find that your own comments seem to come naturally from within. If you find that you are always worried about what you should say next, then you probably just need to listen more. It is well worth the effort for the improvement it will make in your relationships with others and the quality of life in your family. Parents who work on improving their communication skills will naturally teach their children how to communicate better, and their children will benefit from it at home and in their performance in school.

2

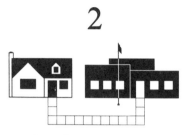

Rules in the Home

The written or unwritten rules that govern how family members interact with each other have a great impact on how well a child does in school. Many important habits and attitudes are learned in the home, and these do not change much when a child gets into the classroom.

Families need to have some kind of rules. These do not need to be complicated, but they should provide clear expectations and consequences. Naturally, each parent grew up with different or even conflicting sets of rules. Then often, without realizing it, they end up sabotaging each other's favorite rules. The kids sit in the middle waiting for the dust to settle. In the meantime they learn not to worry about rules because their parents are not really serious about them anyway.

Every marriage creates a new and in many ways unique family unit. Each parent's background is somewhat different from the other's. Many parents begin rearing their children without recognizing this. Sooner or later, however, they have to come to grips with the different backgrounds and goals of each parent. Instead of waiting until serious problems arise, parents should recognize that a family, like any other group, needs organization. In families, this organization is called *discipline*. Both husband and wife should take the following test and then decide together the appropriate action for them to take in their family on each question.

		Mother's Family	Father's Family
1.	The discipline in my family was handled by:	A. Mother. B. Father. C. Both.	A. Mother. B. Father. C. Both.
2.	Rules for family behavior were set up by:	A. Mother. B. Father. C. Both. D. Family. E. No one.	A. Mother. B. Father. C. Both. D. Family. E. No one.
3.	Mealtimes were pleasant experiences with the family all together.	A. Always. B. Most of the time. C. Never.	A. Always. B. Most of the time. C. Never.
4.	As children, we were encouraged to discuss our feelings openly.	A. Always. B. Usually. C. Seldom. D. Never.	A. Always. B. Usually. C. Seldom. D. Never.
5.	We were expected to tell our parents where we were going before we left and to be in by curfew.	A. Always. B. Usually. C. Seldom. D. Never.	A. Always. B. Usually. C. Seldom. D. Never.
6.	Both of my parents agreed on the rules in our home and consistently saw that they were carried out.	A. Always. B. Usually. C. Seldom. D. Never.	A. Always. B. Usually. C. Seldom. D. Never.
7.	Educational pursuits were important in my family.	A. Very. B. Somewhat. C. Not at all.	A. Very. B. Somewhat. C. Not at all.

	Mother's Family	*Father's Family*
8. Our family did fun things together.	A. Often. B. Sometimes. C. Seldom. D. Never.	A. Often. B. Sometimes. C. Seldom. D. Never.
9. If there was conflict between my parents they:	A. Discussed it. B. Ignored it. C. Were violent.	A. Discussed it. B. Ignored it. C. Were violent.

Once they have some understanding of the differences and similarities in their backgrounds, parents can develop rules for their own family. They need to talk about their expectations for each other and for their children; and for the rules to work, the parents have to be in complete agreement. Any lack of support or agreement on the part of either parent will eventually lead to trouble. If both parents cannot agree on a rule, they should agree not to have it.

Parents need to evaluate their expectations of their children. A child might grow up in a family where productivity is the only measure of a person's worth. The child might never be hugged or told, "I love you because you are my boy." The only positive reinforcement the child might ever receive is that he is a good boy if he scrubs the carrots before bringing them in from the garden.

Because of our society's emphasis on productivity as an indicator of a person's worth, many of our expectations and methods of discipline concentrate on productivity. But children are human beings whose personalities deserve at least as much attention as the fact that the carrots were scrubbed, that they get good grades in school, or that they are on the track team.

Parents should regularly think about the personality development of their children and identify what rules and expectations are needed at that time by each child. Discussing family rules only once is not enough. It should be done periodically until the children are grown. Included in the discussion should be such questions as these: What are our children's strengths and weaknesses? What personality traits are most important for us to develop in our family? What are the needs that each child has in his or her current level of development? In the next short period of time, what specific thing should we concentrate on?

Concentrate on one thing at a time. One child might be having a problem accepting the consequences of his behavior. In that case, you would need to focus your attention on that particular trait. Another child might have a difficult time responding to requests, so you would have to focus your attention on teaching her how to respond appropriately.

Effective discipline begins with the parents. It is really unfair and unreasonable to expect more self-control and change from the children than the parents are willing to give themselves. We have a tendency to spend our time thinking about all the things that children or other people should do to change their behavior. We think about what others should do to make us happy. In reality, we have very little control over others, but we do have control over ourselves. The real reason for any discipline is to develop positive character traits in our children. Our goal is to help them to become independent and self motivated with a strong sense of what is right and wrong.

One of the first things parents need to control is their own emotions. If you are so angry with a child that you cannot deal with the situation calmly, then perhaps you should leave the room until you can control yourself. It is all right to be *angry*, but your *behavior* should be under control. Children should be taught that punishment is a result of breaking family rules, not a result of their parent's anger. Many children feel they are being punished simply because their parents are angry, not because they have done anything to deserve it.

The following example illustrates how a parent could teach this principle to children: One day Brad and his sister Sally had a fight. Both children came running to their mother. Sally said, "Brad hit me." Brad said, "Sally broke my favorite truck." Their mother said, "I understand that you are angry, Brad, but it is wrong to hit your sister. It was also wrong of Sally to break your truck. Let's talk about it and see if we can come to some kind of solution." This mother was making it clear that Brad's feelings were acceptable but that his behavior was unacceptable.

Young children may be able to learn only that their behavior has made their parents angry. That is fine for a first step. By the preteen years, however, children need to know that their behavior brings about clearly defined consequences. However, in far too many instances, children do not know the rules or the consequences for breaking them, and they see any consequences only as a result of the whims or anger of their parents.

A rule is worthless if both parents are not willing and able to enforce it. It is better not to have the rule if they cannot be consistent with it. A rule that isn't followed can set a child up for failure at school.

Consider the following examples and choose what you feel is the most appropriate course of action in each one:

1. Johnny refuses to get up in the morning. You would:
    a. Scream that he is going to be late.
    b. Throw cold water on him.
    c. Rub his back and say, "You deserve more sleep. I'll wake you up again in five minutes."
    d. Get him his own alarm clock and make him responsible for getting himself up.

2. Betty and Sue are arguing over who has to wash the dishes. You would:
    a. Do them yourself.
    b. Spank the girls.
    c. Go away until the fight is over.
    d. Try to discover and treat the real problem.

3. Allan seldom picks up his toys when he is through playing with them. You would:
    a. Pick them up yourself.
    b. Throw them away.

   c. Put them up and tell Allan that because he has been
      irresponsible, he cannot play with his toys for one
      week.
   d. Get a cute toy box so he will want to pick them up.
4.   You have told the kids to go to bed for the fourth time
and they are still up. You would:
   a. Tell them one more time, hoping this time it will
      work.
   b. Let them fall asleep on the floor.
   c. Get angry and spank them.
   d. Devise a plan that would enable you to be firm and
      consistent in your approach to bedtime.
5.   While you were shopping, someone broke the lamp in
the living room. No one will admit to it. You would:
   a. Assume one of the neighbor children did it.
   b. Call a family council and announce that because
      furniture is expensive and must be treated with respect
      and since no one will admit to the incident, there
      will be no dessert for anyone until enough money
      has been saved to pay for the lamp.
   c. Cry.
   d. Get angry and spank everyone.
6.   There is constant bickering about whose turn it is to
take out the garbage. You would:
   a. Devise a work chart where everyone takes turns.
   b. Do it yourself to avoid the argument.
   c. Decide who should do it based on that day's behav-
      ior.
   d. Assign it to one person as a permanent job.
   If your answers were 1-d, 2-d, 3-c or d, 4-d, 5-b, and 6-a,
you are on your way to being able to develop workable rules
in your family.
   The experiences children have with rules in their first five
years as well as the attitudes they develop toward rules will in
large part determine how they will react to rules at school (and
in the community at large). Parents need to teach the following attitudes to their children:
   1.   Rules are necessary.

2. Rules are to help me be free of habits and behaviors that will be destructive to me in the long run.

3. Rules can be challenged as long as I do it in the right way and at an appropriate time.

4. If I challenge a rule, I have the responsibility not only to come up with a better alternative but also to be at least partly responsible for implementing the change if my alternative is accepted.

A few guidelines helpful in setting rules are:

1. Reward and punishment deny children the opportunity to make their own decisions and to be responsible for their own behavior.

2. Natural and logical consequences require children to be responsible for their own behavior.

3. *Natural* consequences are those that permit children to learn from the natural order of the physical world—for example, that not eating is followed by hunger.

4. *Logical* consequences are those that permit children to learn from the reality of the social order. For example, children who do not get up on time may be late to school and have to make up work.

5. For consequences to be effective, children must see them as logical.

6. The purpose of using natural and logical consequences is to motivate children to make responsible decisions, not to force their submission. Consequences are effective only if you avoid having hidden motives of winning and controlling.

7. Be both firm and kind. Firmness refers to your follow-through behavior. Kindness refers to the manner in which you present the choice.

8. Talk less about consequences; act more.

9. When you do things for children that they can do for themselves, you rob them of self-respect and responsibility.

10. There are several differences between punishment and logical consequences. (a) Punishment expresses the power of personal authority; logical consequences express the impersonal reality of the social order. (b) Punishment is rarely related to misbehavior; logical consequences are logically

related to misbehavior. (c) Punishment tells children they are bad; logical consequences imply no element of moral judgment. (d) Punishment focuses on what is past; logical consequences are concerned with present and future behavior. (e) Punishment is associated with a threat, either open or concealed; logical consequences are based on goodwill, not on retaliation. (f) Punishment demands obedience; logical consequences permit choice.

11. Avoid fights; they indicate lack of respect for the other person. Do not give in; that indicates lack of respect for yourself.

12. There are three steps in applying logical consequences: (a) Provide choices and accept the child's decision; use a friendly tone of voice that communicates your goodwill. (b) As you follow through with a consequence, assure children that they may try again later. (c) If the misbehavior is repeated, extend the time that must elapse before the child tries again.

13. Be patient; it will take time for natural and logical consequences to be effective. (Adapted from Rudolf Dreikurs and Loren Grey, *A Parent's Guide to Child Discipline* [New York: Hawthorne Books, 1970].)

One very important habit for a student to develop is that of completing tasks. This skill needs to be learned at home. It is difficult if not impossible to learn it in school. Family rules and traditions help to establish this habit. For example, if a family has the rule that after dinner everyone helps to clean up the table and stack the dishes, the notion begins to sink in that there are certain things that are done before one runs off to have fun. Many small family traditions can teach gradually that certain responsibilities come before personal wants.

I once knew a two-year-old boy named Jonathan who was fascinated with the mechanism that operated the living room drapes. His wise parents found a way to reinforce this mechanism so that a two-year-old could do no damage to it and gave him the responsibility of being the family drape operator. It was his job to open the drapes every morning and to close them at night. If there was a reason to open or close the drapes any other time, Jonathan had to be asked to do the job. He realized at an early age that he had responsibilities in the family and that he had an important place in the family structure. As he grew older, he was given additional assignments. His next job was to order milk from the milkman. He was four at the time. He was to put the color-coded tags on the milkbox every other day to tell the milkman what products to leave for the family. The rule was that they could not purchase milk at the store. If Jonathan did not accomplish his task correctly, the whole family had to suffer. He learned that his behavior not only had consequences for himself but for others as well. One of the devices that helped to reinforce this notion with Jonathan was a daily chart. Every night as a part of his bedtime ritual, one of his parents would ask him if he had accomplished the goals that were listed on his chart. If he had accomplished a goal, he could choose a colored sticker to put on the appropriate square on his chart. His first chart had these items on it: 1. Open the drapes. 2. Dress myself. 3. Pick up all my toys at night. 4. Close the drapes. As other assignments were given, a new chart was made. This also taught Jonathan about regular reporting and evaluation of performance.

For older children, another approach is very effective. After any assignment is completed, or once a week, a parent should sit down with a child and ask three questions: (1) What do you like most about the job (or jobs) you have done; (2) What do you like least about what you were able to do; (3) What would you do differently next time? You should make note of what the child liked least and also what he would do differently. Next week you should be able to make positive comments about his efforts to do a better job. If you establish this kind of routine early and make the rule for yourself that you will not say anything negative to a child until after you have said at least three positive things, you will find that your child has developed a fine sense of responsibility and self-evaluation.

One of the major problems with many of the teenagers I meet with is that they have the notion that their behavior has no consequences for anyone but themselves, and even the connection between consequences and their own behavior is tenuous. They believe that anything bad that happens to them is because someone is "out to get them," not because they made a wrong choice or behaved badly.

On one of my recordings of parental interactions with children is a choice example of how to teach children to ignore rules. It starts out with a conversation between a mother and several of her friends in the living room. At one point the mother says, "Please don't touch the TV, David." After further conversation she says, "David, now don't play with the TV, please." Several minutes later she says, "David, I don't want to have to tell you again not to play with the TV. Leave it alone." Then still later she says, "David, I am telling you for the last time to leave the TV alone." Each time she speaks, there is a little more anger and frustration in her voice. Eventually, in a much louder voice, she says, "David, you are really going to be in trouble if you don't stop doing that." Some more time passes and finally she says in anguish, "Oh, David! Now look what you've done!"

In this interchange and many others like it, David learned some significant principles:

1. Do not listen to mother (or any adult). She doesn't really mean what she says.

2. Do whatever you want because there are not going to be any consequences for your behavior.

Parents are wise to repeat a request only once, to give their child the benefit of the doubt. After the second statement, the parent should *do* something. Parents do not have to be violent or mean, but they must *do something*. David's mother needed only to pick David up and put him in a different room. After several years of such consequences, children learn that they need to listen to parents because they are going to say something only twice and then they will do something. If the parents do something different each time, they leave the child wondering what is going to happen. Usually children will decide that they do not want to find out what will happen. At times it may even be wise to ask a child if he has understood your request. Do not be satisfied with a response like, "Yes, I heard you." Instead, say something like, "I want to make sure that I said what I meant. Would you please tell me what you understood me to say." That way you can listen to what the child says and make correction if he has not understood.

The following interaction between a teacher and a group of students who wanted permission to eat their lunch in the classroom while they worked on a project is a good example:

Student: Miss Jones, we would like to eat here in the classroom every day this week so that we can finish our project. Would that be okay?

Teacher: That would be fine, but you must understand that if you choose to leave a mess, you have also chosen to eat your lunch in the cafeteria. Now, please tell me your understanding of our agreement.

Student: You said that if we make a mess you won't let us eat in the classroom anymore.

Teacher: No, that is not quite what I meant. It is not up to me what happens, it is up to you. It is your choice. If you choose to make a mess then you have also chosen to eat in the cafeteria, and I believe in honoring your choices. Now, please tell me how you understand the situation.

Student: Okay. If we make a mess you will take it from that that we want to eat in the cafeteria rather than the classroom and we will get exactly what we want.

Teacher: Exactly.

In this example, the teacher was careful to make sure that her message was well understood. She felt it was important that these sixth graders understand that they were indicating their choice by their behavior and that they would be held accountable for that choice.

Families need to meet together regularly to discuss their interactions with one another and to clarify what rules are a part of the family system. The family meeting or family council is not a time to hear a lecture from Mother or Father. Family councils promote a feeling of oneness in a family. All family members come to know their individual importance to the group. They realize that their opinions and actions really matter. No family is immune to problems, but many problems can be avoided if a family will meet together regularly to discuss how they should interact with one another, what the rules are, and the consequences for breaking the rules. Each member of the family should help decide on those rules and consequences. The complexity of modern life and the diversity of family members' needs ensure that problems will be plentiful. Successful families have no magical power; they have developed effective ways to deal with their problems. Successful families are always trying to start things. Failing families are always trying to stop things. Effective family problem-solving requires the following:

1. *Open communication.* Free exchange of ideas and information are vital to solving problems. All members of the family should contribute to the discussion and parents need to support and encourage participation by everyone.

2. *Central leadership.* One person needs to lead the discussion. Different people may lead the family in solving different problems, according to their expertise. At times, one of the children might serve as the discussion leader.

3. *Acceptance of conflicting ideas.* Conflicting ideas are often helpful in solving problems because they tend to produce solutions that will work for everyone, not just a few. So, family members should be willing to hear and accept ideas that are different from their own.

4. *Agreement on group goals.* Family members must be committed to solving certain agreed-upon problems, even though they may have different ideas about how to solve them. This leads to family unity and cooperation.

As a family continues to develop problem-solving skills, problems become easier to handle, not because the nature of problems change, but because the family's ability to deal effectively with problems increases. (Adapted from Irving Tallman, "The Family As a Small Problem Solving Group," *Journal of Marriage and the Family*, February 1974.)

An agenda for a typical family council might include these parts:

1. Opening. This might be a story, remarks, prayer, song, or whatever fits your family.

2. Statement of purpose. You might say something like, "We are meeting to decide on a regular time to have a family council."

3. Suggestions. Encourage every person to share his or her feelings.

4. Comments on each suggestion. Example: "I can tell you are really thinking." "You have some good ideas." "That's an interesting comment." Make sure any comment you give is positive. This will encourage your children to voice their opinions and eases the disappointment if their particular choice is not adopted by the family. Be sure to write down every idea and suggestion.

5. Making decisions. You can vote on decisions by a raise of hands, by secret ballot, or simply by asking all family members to state how they feel as a result of the discussion. Make clear that the results of any voting will be taken into consideration by you and your spouse when you meet in executive session. In other words, the decisions are still made or ratified by Mom and Dad, taking into consideration the vote of the family.

6. Time for problems or plans to be presented to the family. Planning a family calendar for the week is a good idea.

7. Closing. Include remarks, a song, or a prayer adapted to your family.

8. Refreshments. Refreshments don't need to be fancy, but they make a good ending.

Family councils give family members an opportunity to talk and work together. Parents can share their ideas and values with their children and teach basic principles of conflict resolution and problem solving. The parents are the executive committee of the family, and they make the decisions as they meet together regularly. If they are wise, they will listen to what the children say and incorporate what they have heard into their decisions so that the children know that their ideas have been considered. The children's contributions can be very important, and parents need to listen to them carefully. Parents do not, however, need to agree. Children will understand that they can't have their own way all the time as long as they feel that they have been listened to and that some of their ideas have influenced family decisions. Family rules need to be constantly clarified, discussed, and posted so they will be read and understood.

A friend once told me about a city that had a mystery speed limit on all of the streets. Every morning the chief of police would call the mayor to find out what the speed limit was. If the city was doing well financially, there was no limit. If the city was in trouble, the limit was very low. The people became more and more afraid to drive because they never knew what they could get away with. They didn't know what the limits were. That is what often happens to children. They find that if their parents are feeling good, they can get away with almost anything. If their parents are having a bad day, they could be punished for almost anything. It is this lack of consistency that makes life difficult for children. I know of parents who, according to all the theories, are really doing everything wrong. But they do everything so clearly and consistently and are so united that the children do very well.

It is even a good idea for families to write a family constitution. As soon as a couple get married, they should sit down and talk about what kind of system they want to have in their home and what kind of rules they think are important enough to commit themselves to. They can also talk about the kinds of traditions they want to create in their family for special occasions or to give their family a special character.

One rule that should be a part of every family constitution from the first day of marriage is this: anytime anyone goes someplace, they notify a member of the family where they are going and when they will return. If plans change, they will notify a responsible member of the family. If they cannot notify anyone, they must stick to the original plan.

Usually the first person to break this rule is one of the parents. If the parents can faithfully live this rule, I guarantee that they will have fewer problems with their teenagers. Usually children will not really be aware of this rule until they become teenagers, who have more mobility than small children. Then, they immediately see the rule as an indication of their parents' lack of trust in them or their parents' desire to control them. If you can say to your teenagers, "This has been a rule in our family since the day we got married. We all live according to this rule," you will have a much easier time dealing with them.

Another rule that can help teach children to be responsible for their own behavior is this one: Taking care of the house, inside and out, is a responsibility shared equally by every member of the family. We will meet regularly to give everyone part of this responsibility according to each person's ability.

You need to explain that Mom and Dad may seem to be responsible for everything, but that is only because until the children are old enough to do their part, the parents have to do the job. If Mother has accepted the responsibility for doing the wash, or if this responsibility is passed around, it should not include gathering up the dirty clothes from all over the house. Dirty clothes should go in a certain place, and any clothes not put in that place should not be washed. A three-year-old is old enough to understand this. If a child comes to you one morning and says, "I don't have any clean clothes to wear to school," you should say only, "I am sorry about that, but it is not my problem. You knew where to put your clothes if you wanted them washed. You chose not to put them there, so you have chosen to have dirty clothes." Older children might even have to take their clothes to the laundromat and pay to have them washed. This would teach them to be responsible for their own behavior and not to expect the whole world to cater to them.

Parents should spend twelve years teaching children how to clean and take care of their rooms. On a child's twelfth birthday, they should present a certificate that reads: "On your twelfth birthday, we, your parents, hereby grant you the right to be completely in charge of your own room. We will not enter it to clean it, to retrieve dirty clothes from it, or to make your bed. You are in charge. If we don't like what we see there, we will ask you to keep the door shut so that we don't have to look at it."

Many parents cannot bring themselves to do this because of their need to be seen as the parents of neat children, not because of any real principle. This action on the part of parents can help to teach children how to deal with things that are their responsibility. They may not do very well with it for a while. In order for this to work of course, two things must happen during those first twelve years. First, the child must be taught correctly how to take care of a room. Second, the parents must present a good example in how they take care of their own room.

Similarly, parents need to make a clear rule about pets. This rule should say something like this: If a child has a pet he will be completely responsible for it. The parents will remind him of his responsibility occasionally, but if the life or health of the pet is in danger because of the child's irresponsibility, another home will be found for the pet.

This rule will help children learn to be responsible for a pet. The pet will be protected, and the parents will avoid becoming the ones who take care of it. In many families, the mother somehow gets stuck with the job of taking care of all the pets, and she will often not really understand how this happened to her.

Sometime between the ages of ten and twelve, each child should become responsible for providing a meal for the entire family once a week. This might start out with getting out the milk and cereal for breakfast. The next step might be soup and sandwiches for lunch. Then they can try preparing a full dinner. There will be far less complaining about meals when the children know that they are responsible for some of them. Knowing how to prepare meals will also help your children when they are ready to leave home for college, marriage, or career.

Work on reinforcing the positive behaviors and attitudes that you have decided are important and ignore most of the negative behavior. If you are continually giving children attention for positive things they have done, then you have a foundation to sit down with them and occasionally discuss some of the negative things they need to change. Discuss their negative behaviors as a coach and friend who will help them to change rather than as dictator who demands change "or else."

Establish a training program in your home. As you do so, one of your basic assumptions ought to be this: Anytime children do something wrong, they must not know how to do it right. Do not criticize them—teach them!

If your six-year-old runs to tell you that your four-year-old is making a mess in the living room, stop and remind the child of this assumption. The six-year-old saw the four-year-old doing something wrong, so it is the six-year-old's responsibility to find a way to teach the four-year-old how to take care of the living room. You did not see the four-year-old, so his behavior is not your responsibility. Your main effort should be to help your six-year-old deal with the situation and develop a plan. You might suggest that the six-year-old go back to the living room and tell the younger child that they can play a game of picking up the paper that has been thrown around the room because that is how they should take care of the living room. The parent should then stay out of the situation except to give support and advice to the older child, if and when the child returns for further help. This way you teach children not to criticize and yell at each other but to help and teach each other. You also teach them that they are not going to be able to get their brothers and sisters in trouble by telling on them.

In establishing any kind of training program, you should carefully consider the consequences and rewards you will use. Consequences need to be as closely related to the offense as possible and not too overwhelming. If you tell a child that he will be grounded for a month, you have just lost your ability to have much influence on that child for the next month. Grounding should last only for a day or two, or possibly a week if the situation is severe. You don't want your children to think that they are so far in the hole that there is no hope.

If they do, they may decide to continue with their negative behavior. Each child is different. One child might consider spending fifteen minutes alone in his room the worst punishment in the world. Another child might enjoy it. You have to know your children and think about what will work with each one.

You do not want to have to continually use rewards and consequences to maintain good behavior. But you might have to carefully use these tools to get new behavior started or old behavior stopped. Any new behavior is very fragile. It has to be nourished and encouraged if it is to become strong and sturdy. Eventually you want to reach the point where the behavior is firmly established and rewards itself, with only occasional reinforcement from you. An important principle here is that the rules may stay the same but the system of training, rewarding, or punishing the behavior associated with those rules may change as the child grows more responsible. This is why some schools actually create problems by trying to systematize the "discipline" program throughout the school. This does not usually allow for individual differences and growth. A particular reward system may be needed to get a new behavior started, but if you continue to use that reward system, it can become self-defeating. Similarly, you may need to use a particular consequence to get a behavior stopped, but in order to keep that behavior stopped, you may change the system or even eliminate it, at least until the behavior shows up again.

I knew a teenager who wanted to become a great organist. His mother complained often that she could not get him to practice regularly, and he even reported that the constant hassle from his mother was beginning to make him think he would simply stop playing completely. I suggested that the parents needed to allow their son to be responsible for his own practice time. Both parents were certain that the only thing that would keep him practicing was their constant pressure. But they were getting a lot more arguing than practicing. I asked the boy how serious he was about wanting to succeed with his music. He said he really wanted to but just had problems getting around to doing the kind of practice that was required. He knew he should, but when his parents nagged him about it, he stopped practicing just to spite them.

After some discussion, we wrote up a contract. He was very proud to have saved $500. He agreed to put the money into a savings account with his name and my name on it. The contract specified that any day he did not practice, I could withdraw $50. Anytime his parents even mentioned practice, they had to deposit $50. After several months of successful practicing with no deposits or withdrawals, we decided that the contract was no longer needed, and the young man put his money back into his own account. He had proven to his parents that he could be responsible without their constant nagging. He wanted to achieve the goal, but he needed to develop internal motivation.

Structure is important because it prevents confusion. For example, if children know what time they must go to bed every night, they get used to the idea and can plan on it happening. If bedtime is viewed as an important event and given proper attention, it can be a loving, nurturing experience. The children will see that this event is important enough to have your undivided attention and will be more likely to cooperate. One-half hour before bedtime, turn off the television and put away all books and toys, have the children get ready for bed, and spend a few minutes with each child for prayers or conversation. Being firm and consistent is an important key to fostering good feelings at bedtime.

All children are free agents, and they may choose, in spite of all you do, to do whatever they like. How well you can implement family rules will depend on the quality of the relationship you build with your children and the unity of you and your spouse.

Any social system, including family rules, must be backed up by power and authority. Parents have power only if they agree on what the rules are. A father may think that he has authority, but if he is using that authority without the complete support of the mother, there is no real power behind the rules in that family. Anarchy and chaos reign in the minds of the children. A father may be strong enough to suppress discipline problems for some time, but eventually they will become uncontrollable.

That is why parents should spend some time talking about what they want and what their expectations are. Together they should come up with a few clear, well-defined rules and then teach those rules to their children through word and example. This will help children become more responsible both at home and at school.

3

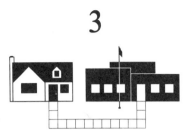

Emotional Climate in the Home

How well children do in school is related to their self-esteem. Self-esteem is a gift children get from their parents, and it is based on the emotional climate in the home. It should not be left to chance.

A positive emotional climate begins with the quality of the relationship between the parents. That does not mean that the relationship will be free of disagreements. Any meaningful relationship will have some conflict. We should not expect to have a relationship free of conflict but should instead learn to deal with conflict creatively and constructively. Being able to communicate, to set a few clear rules, and to be as consistent as possible are all important. But the most important thing is how the parents feel about each other and how that feeling is expressed in their behavior.

Children are great observers, but they are often poor interpreters. They may interpret certain behaviors as meaning that Mom and Dad hate each other, when just the opposite is the case. Parents need to be careful about how children perceive their relationship. Often it is necessary for parents to reassure their children about the depth and stability of their marriage. They may say something like, "You know we have been arguing the last couple of days, but that doesn't mean we don't love each other. We have just been trying to agree on what we should do. We still love each other very much, and our marriage is strong." This teaches children that conflicts sometimes occur but that love is more important than conflicts.

Another important part of a family's emotional climate is how family members talk to each other. Often parents fail to mention their children's achievements or good behavior but talk only about their children's mistakes and problems. Their children soon learn to expect this and may even learn that the only way they can get some kind of emotional reaction from their parents is to make them angry.

Everyone needs and longs for emotional involvement with others. The opposite of love is not hate; it is apathy or indifference. When children feel that they are not getting the love they need, they may not know how to communicate their feelings. They need to be taught how to invite or request closeness. A parent might say, "When you feel you need some hugging, come and tell me." Any number of simple clues can be taught to children so they can tell you what they need. Unfortunately, children usually learn the negative things they can do to get an immediate emotional response from their parents. For most children, being yelled at is better than being ignored.

Some theories of behavior suggest that if people feel something, they have the right to express it fully. This is incorrect. Successful family life requires a positive emotional climate in the home, and this climate is maintained by controlling the intensity of anger, frustration, and tension and introducing more positive feelings.

A fourteen-year-old named Tom has parents who are divorced. Because of the fighting that went on before the divorce, Tom had learned that the way to get what he wanted from others was to shout them down, sometimes using foul and abusive language. His mother recognized that to help her son overcome this problem, she would have to do two things: First, she would have to refuse to fight with him when he was angry; and second, she would have to help increase the positive experiences in her son's life. Needless to say, this required a great deal of discipline on her part.

The next time Tom gave one of his usual performances, his mother, refusing to give him the negative attention he was after, locked herself in the bedroom, took a bath, and went to bed. The next morning Tom came to the bedroom door and said, "Mom, I'm sorry about the way I acted last night. I really love you." She responded, "Son, I love you too, and I understand your frustration. I wonder if you understand how it makes me feel when you act that way?" When he said he thought he knew, she said, "Well, could we please think of some other way to deal with your anger and frustration?"

This was the beginning of real communication between mother and son. When parents are able to communicate calmly and honestly with their children, they build a positive home environment, and both parents and children tend to be more cooperative with each other. This usually requires parents to control their own emotions (or rather their behavior based on their emotions). Parents should avoid shouting and violence and instead practice expressing their emotions calmly.

Self-esteem is closely related to whether or not children feel accepted by their father. Mothers are usually better at communicating caring and acceptance than fathers. There is evidence that children who feel loved and accepted by their fathers are less likely to become involved with drugs or alcohol. Fathers who develop close emotional and physical relationships with their children somehow create strengths in those youngsters that make them less likely to become involved in deviant behavior.

Often the weak link in the family chain is the father. Either he is not often physically present or he does not contribute much to the development of his children.

I remember a father who spent time with his two sons only by taking them to hockey games. He loved the fights that often broke out on the ice and often screamed encouragement for them. Why, then, was he so surprised when his boys became violent and destructive as they moved into their teenage years? They had been taught that this was the way to earn support and love from their father. Children learn positive character traits and high self-esteem from parents who listen, take time to share their feelings, help them become involved in constructive activities, and call attention to the children's strengths and successes before they warmly but firmly confront them with their mistakes.

To make a brief assessment of your children's self-esteem ask yourself the following questions about each of them:

1. Does my child have a good attitude toward work? Does he find satisfaction in completing tasks and in doing a good job?

2. Does my child make good use of his natural talents and abilities?

3. Does my child have a wholesome attitude toward sex and his sexual feelings?

4. Does my child have a healthy appreciation of money, and is he able to handle money matters adequately?

5. Am I able to communicate religious values to my child, and is he receptive?

6. When there is a difference of opinion, are we able to sit down together, discuss it, and come to a workable conclusion for both of us?

7. Does my child have a good sense of responsibility around the home?

8. Are expressions of love and appreciation an important part of the relationship between me and my child?

9. Is my child beginning to grasp the reasons for rules he is asked to follow?

10. Is my child strong enough to stand up for his own beliefs and not feel obliged to "follow the crowd"?

11. Does my child accept and respect the standards of our family?

12. Does my child understand what is meant by "talking our feelings out" as opposed to "acting them out in inappropriate behavior"?

13. Does my child have the ability to laugh, to find humor in his mistakes, and to keep going when the going gets rough?

14. Does my child have friends who enrich his life and encourage him to be successful and happy?

15. Does my child work to the best of his intellectual ability?

16. Does my child have good control over his eating and sleeping habits?

17. Does my child treat his brothers and sisters with respect?

18. Do I care what happens to my child?

Several years ago a program was started to help prevent drug abuse among teenagers. Those who planned the program must have felt that the key to solving the problem was to scare teenagers to death. They had little concern about the accuracy of the information presented as long as it painted a frightening enough picture. Teenagers do not respond to such an approach. They usually feel that they will never have to bear the consequences of their behavior. Instead of being frightened, many felt challenged to try drugs to see if the information was true. Many of the young people became adept at spotting the information that was not true. As a result, they became reluctant to believe what *was* true. They learned that they could not trust adults.

It is important that parents do not try this approach. Parents must resist any inclination to use false or overstated information in order to motivate their children. Honesty is always the best policy.

One of the most important elements in a positive emotional climate is cooperation. Without cooperation, no organization would be able to exist. There could be no communication. Occupations, education, and economic exchange could not exist. Without cooperation, civilization would crumble. Cooperation is best taught in the home.

To get a feeling for what kinds of cooperation to expect from children, consider the following chart:

Cooperation from Children

Behavior	Weeks Old
Responds to smiling and talking	6
Knows mother	12
Shows marked interest in father	14
Is sober with strangers	16
Withdraws from strangers	32

Behavior	Weeks Old
Responds to inhibitory words (such as "no")	51

Behavior	Years	Months
Is no longer shy toward strangers	1	3
Is interested in and treats other children like objects rather than like other people		
Enjoys imitating adult activities		
Plays alone	1	6
Brings objects to adults		
Begins to understand private ownership	1	9
Wants to participate in household activities		
Has interest in and watches other children	2	
Plays with other children		
Is dependent and passive in relation to adults		
Is shy toward strangers		
Is not sociable; lacks social interest	2	3
Shows ritualistic behavior	2	6
Is imperious, domineering		
Begins to resist adult influence; wants to be independent		
Fights with children of own age		
Refuses to share toys; ignores requests		

Behavior	*Years*	*Months*
Begins to accept suggestions	3	
Identifies with mother		
Likes to relive babyhood		
Is independent of mother at times		
Tends to establish social contacts with adults		
Imitates actions of others		
Begins strong friendships with peers with discrimination against others	3	6
Is assertive, boastful	4	
Has definite preference for peers		
Tries to get attention: shows off		
Tends to be obedient, cooperative; wants to please	5	
Seeks approval; avoids disapproval of adults		
Shows preference for children of own age		
Shows protective, mothering attitude toward younger siblings		
Is sensitive to feelings of others	6	
Has strong desire to be with father and do things together (especially boys)		
Insists on being first in everything with peers		
Bosses and teases younger siblings		
Likes to pretend in social play		

(Adapted from Brian Sutton-Smith, Child Psychology.)

Behavior	*Years*	*Months*
Shows compliance in family relations	7	
Wants to be good		
Begins to discriminate between sexes		
Forms close friendships with others of the same sex	8	
Sex differences obvious (girls giggle, whisper; boys wrestle, roughhouse)		
Enjoys belonging to clubs		
Sex differences more pronounced; girls show more poise, folk wisdom, interest in family, and personal appearance	10	

(Adapted from Brian Sutton-Smith, *Child Psychology*.)

Parents can make it impossible for their children to learn how to cooperate by developing a climate of competition in the home. Children will face enough competition outside of the home without having to face it at home as well. In fact, parents should work to control some of the intense competition that their children may face at school.

Children under the age of twelve should not be forced to deal with the "win at all costs" philosophy that is so rampant today in competitive sports and in some of our classrooms. Sports programs for children under twelve are good for them if the following rules are adhered to:

1. Anyone who wants to play can play.
2. Each participant plays an equal amount of time.
3. No awards are given for winning a game. Awards are given only for participating, meeting personal or team goals, and making a good effort.

Children need recreation, but they do not need the pressure of winning in order to build the egoes of coaches or parents. During middle or later adolescence, they are much better able to deal with that kind of pressure.

This same problem occurs in classrooms where teachers are allowed to assign grades using the curve. There is no justification for such a practice, and parents should make sure that it is stopped. Schools should use criterion-referenced grading, where the criteria for receiving a certain grade are specified clearly at the beginning of the course. The criteria should be challenging, but if every student meets the criteria for an A, then every student should receive an A. To arbitrarily say that only 10 percent may receive an A and 10 percent must fail is the height of educational stupidity.

Parents must make sure that they do not use competition as a way to motivate their children in the home. Children should not be compared to others. They should be taught to measure their own progress based on the goals they have set for themselves. If you have children who go to the same school, they will probably have the same teacher at some time. When a teacher says, "Oh, I taught your older sister," your child should say, "That is true, but I am not my sister. I am unique, and what you know about my sister may not apply to me."

All people have their own strengths and weaknesses, and parents need to understand the uniqueness of each of their children. It is easy to fall into the trap of using competition to motivate children, both at home and at school. There are even some well-developed myths that support this approach.

Myth 1: Our society is highly competitive, and children must be taught to succeed in a "survival of the fittest" world. Many advocates of competition insist that schools and homes must emphasize a dog-eat-dog theory of survival in the occupational world. To be better than the Joneses is the deepest desire of such people. Yet human interaction, in our society as well as in all other societies, is not competitive but cooperative. We are a social species. Cooperation is a biological necessity for humans. Without cooperation, society could not exist. There could be no communication, exchange of goods and services, entertainment, or education. Social psychology suggests that competition is a very small part of interacting with others.

Myth 2: Achievement and motivation depend upon competing with others. The appeal of this myth to those who want to be great is overwhelming. They want to set the world straight and show us a better way of life. However, achievement does not occur because of competition. Performance can actually suffer under competition, and a person who is superior in one situation may be markedly inferior in another. Competition usually decreases the quality of a student's work and will in no way determine who is the best person to achieve under a variety of conditions. The only children motivated by competition are those who believe they have a good chance of winning. Competition is threatening and discouraging to those who believe they cannot win, and many children will withdraw psychologically or physically in competition. Children are motivated when a goal is desirable, possible, challenging, concrete, and requires positive interaction with others.

Myth 3: Competition builds character and toughness for life in the real world. Underneath each competitive athletic program is the belief that competition builds character. The thinking seems to be that if one competes on the football field, one builds the character to win in Congress! Ogilvie and Tutko (1971) spent eight years studying the effects of competition on the personality. They focused upon athletic competition, as "a young athlete often must face in hours or days the kind of pressure that occurs in the life of the achievement-oriented man over several years." They found no evidence that competition in athletics builds character; indeed, they found evidence that athletic competition limits growth in some areas. Many athletes have a low interest in receiving support and concern from others, a low need to take care of others, and a low need for affiliation with others. These are not the traits needed to succeed in our cooperative society.

Myth 4: Students prefer competitive situations. How easy it is to believe that competition is used in schools because students demand it! Children seem to enjoy competition as long as they are winning, but they absolutely refuse to participate in competition when they feel they will not win. Recent studies have shown that students prefer cooperatively structured instruction to competitive instruction, especially if they have had experience in cooperative learning situations. In one study 100 percent of the sixth-grade children who participated in a cooperatively structured science unit stated they preferred a cooperative classroom structure.

Myth 5: Competition builds self-confidence and self-esteem. The winner must be full of self-confidence and be proud! Yet if that is true, why do so many winners have psychological problems, especially in adapting to situations in which winning is no longer relevant? The truth seems to be that competition often leads to insecurity and low self-esteem (the unforgivable sin is finishing second), and most students experience failure most of the time under competition. It is impossible to make all students winners using a competitive approach.

Of course, competition is not inherently evil and need not always be avoided. In the home, however, it should be avoided as much as possible. Under the appropriate circumstances, competition can be exciting and enjoyable, whether the participants win or lose. Children need to learn how to recognize those times when competition may be of value and enjoyable and gain the perspective needed to choose whether or not to compete. (Adapted from David W. and Roger T. Johnson, *Learning Together and Alone* [Englewood Cliffs: Prentice-Hall, 1975], pp. 45-49.)

A football coach even created a system of managing a high-school football team that eliminated the negative aspects of team competition and helped each team member to grow individually. After each game, he asked the team members to help him set goals for each team member and the team as a whole. His job as coach was to plan practice sessions so that these goals could be met. During an actual game, the coach would not become involved. He would make a decision or intervene only if he thought that some member of the team was in danger. The team members were to put into practice what they had learned during the week. After using this system for a while, the coach found that the young men on the team became much more interested in reaching their goals than in "beating" the other team. In fact, they began to make friends with team members from other schools. Destructive rivalries disappeared, and each player showed significant progress academically as well as physically. The players had learned how to set goals and compete with themselves rather than with others. The win-at-all-costs philosophy so prevalent in school sports is not necessary, and in my view it should never be allowed.

The junior-high principals of one of the largest school districts in Utah saw that interschool sports competition was destructive for junior-high students, and that it did not meet the real needs the students had. They proposed that all interschool athletic competition be eliminated and that the money be spent on a comprehensive intramural program that emphasized participation by as many students as possible. The proposal was defeated at a school-board meeting because of pressure from a vocal minority of parents. Most of the parents did not understand what was really important for their children or just didn't bother to get involved.

As children grow, parents need to teach them to cooperate . They can do this by having an appropriate set of rules to follow and teaching communication skills. The following information gives specific examples of how children might cooperate and why:

Behavior. Child did chore.

Reason. Parents were specific in their instructions about what needed to be done and when.

Explanation. When the parents asked the child to do the task they (1) made sure the child understood the instructions by giving them in a way the child could understand; (2) made sure the physical conditions were right; (3) took into consideration the age and physical capabilities of the child; (4) gave honest praise for a good job.

Behavior. Child worked until task was completed.

Reason. Parents had helped the child feel a sense of accomplishment for his work and produced an atmosphere where work was rewarding.

Explanation. Parents showed by their example how to follow through and complete tasks. They were free with their praise. They were thorough in teaching what was expected to finish a job. They had worked to create a positive feeling with the child. They had given much positive feedback.

Behavior. Child cooperated in working with others.

Reason. Parents had given the child real responsibility and taught him the value of work.

Explanation. Parents gave the child many opportunities to work with other family members. They told him what was expected, praised his good work, and were specific about what each child was to do.

Behavior. Child participated well in family activities.

Reason. Parents made the family activities fun and made each person feel like an important part of the family.

Explanation. Parents allowed the children to help choose the activity, took into account the age and interests of the children, and creativity in carrying out the activities.

The next examples show how a poor emotional climate provokes bad behavior from a child:

Behavior. Job never started.

Reason. Lack of knowledge of what was expected.

Parent's responsibility. Full details of job not explained.

Child's responsibility. Details explained but forgotten. Did not pay attention to instructions.

Behavior. Job started but not finished or not done correctly.

Reason. Lack of knowledge of how to do what was expected.

Parent's responsibility. Instructions too complicated to remember. Unawareness of child's lack of knowledge.

Child's responsibility. Did not use available sources of information.

Behavior. Crying, fussing, and whining.

Reason. Lack of ability.

Parent's responsibility. Delegated job that required more skill, training, or ability than the child had. Unaware of child's illness, worry, or fatigue.

Child's responsibility. Did not take trouble to practice.

Behavior. Ignored instructions and job.

Reason. Lack of desire to do what was expected.

Parent's responsibility. Lack of friendly feeling toward child.

Child's responsibility. Angry with parent. Didn't feel like working. Nobody else was doing the work or did not see any sense in the job. (Adapted from Irman H. Gross et al., *Management for Modern Families*, 4th ed. [Englewood Cliffs, N.J.: Prentice-Hall, 1980], p. 344.)

The following guidelines will help children develop their self-esteem:

1. Respect children's occasional need to say no but continue to guide them through the behavior you expect of them. Remember that it is better to channel or direct their behavior than it is to confront it. Channel children's defiant acts into acceptable outlets. Invent games that allow both of you to get tasks done.

2. Give positive suggestions instead of direct orders.

3. During children's first three years, try not to cause them undue stress about toilet training, mealtime, or independence.

4. Provide experiences for children that offset their feelings of incompetence. Give them tasks that they can master and then be sure to praise them for their success. To help your children succeed in their tasks, you may need to provide stools to reach things, low hooks to hang things on, unbreakable dishes, and so on.

5. Give your children some nursery-school experience around the age of three in a school that is well structured and teaches specific skills rather than merely baby-sitting.

6. Recognize that young children's emotional attachment to the opposite-sexed parent provides them with their

first attempt at establishing a romantic relationship. If handled wisely, this attachment acts as an experience upon which the child builds in adolescence. Do not make them feel guilty about their attachment, and do not accentuate sexual feelings by seductive behavior. Avoid teasing your children about their bodies or about sex. Don't expose them to nudity of opposite-sexed family members. Also, don't let them bathe or sleep with opposite-sexed members of the family.

Drawing the line on these things with calm firmness will help children feel safe with their emerging sexual feelings. It allows them to say, "My feelings are all right. There is nothing wrong with me for having them."

7. When your children begin to think more about themselves than about you (around age five and a half in girls and age six in boys) be firm but understanding. Their need to think of themselves first does not mean that you should constantly give in to them. But you shouldn't make them feel guilty about their self-absorption.

8. Help your children understand their conscience. The conscience begins to take shape around age six, even though the sense of right and wrong is developing earlier. The conscience is made up of the moral standards a child absorbs from the family. If a child takes something that does not belong to him, talk to him privately about it. Help him to make restitution without shame or humiliation. Often children can perform some kind of service for the person from whom they took something. This helps them feel better about themselves while teaching in a positive way that stealing is wrong. Children should not be made to feel bad about something they have done because their moral sense is not yet fully developed.

9. Help your children develop friendships with other children. Around age six, a child moves from total dependence on the family and begins to value the qualities of peers. Children who have friends feel better about themselves than those who do not, and children whose interests and values are different from those of their peers are likely to feel isolated and of less worth. From six years into adolescence, children need

more and more social support from others whose values match their own. Wise parents will provide group activities for children so that they have the opportunity to develop positive relationships. Too often, this is left to chance.

10. Be a good role model to your children. Children between the ages of six and twelve need an adult role model of the same sex so they will learn how to function as a man or a woman when they are older.

Love your children just because they are your children, not for anything they have done. Children between the ages of six and twelve especially need this unconditional love.

Here are a few special guidelines for relating well to adolescents.

1. Respect adolescents' privacy.

2. Make your home attractive. Adolescents are sensitive to their friend's feelings about their home and parents, even though they themselves do not always look their best.

3. Keep your supervision subtle and yet do not neglect it.

4. Avoid making adolescents feel guilty about growing up—about such things as body development, new feelings, friends, dates, or growing independence.

5. Maintain a sense of humor and open communication.

6. Discuss with your adolescents the changes and pressures they may be facing.

7. Discuss with younger siblings your adolescents changing needs.

8. Listen with all your heart to adolescents' feelings and points of view without criticism or evaluation. If you have concerns about any of the feelings or thoughts expressed, wait at least twenty-four hours before discussing them.

9. Establish basic family rules and expectations in a manner that allows for input from each family member.

10. Help adolescents feel competent and successful.

11. Provide a safe climate in the home where adolescents share and try out new behaviors. Provide positive feedback on these behaviors.

By following these guidelines, you will help your children gain self-respect, and this will help them at school.

When children are unsuccessful in building self-respect, they do different things to deal with it. They may become defensive in order to cover up their feelings of inadequacy. They may come to believe that they really are inadequate and that they always will be. Or they retreat into fantasies that block out the rejections they suffer.

What they do depends upon their temperament, role models, experience, and learning. These psychological defenses are weapons against anxiety, fear, insecurity, or inadequacy. Their purpose is to help children maintain their integrity. Most defenses are rooted in a child's belief that he is bad, unlovable, and unworthy. Domination by parents destroys children's self-esteem, courage, and confidence. To build self-esteem, you must use rewards and clear, logical consequences.

Using the chart on this page, you can get a clear picture of what your children will attempt to do based on their self-esteem and ability. The chart includes a list of tasks the child might attempt, a scale to measure the child's general ability, and a scale to measure the child's fear of failure (the opposite of self-esteem).

Tasks	Ability	Fear of Failure
Task 10 *(impossible)*	10 *(high)*	10 *(high)*
Task 9	9	9
Task 8	8	8
Task 7	7	7
Task 6	6	6
Task 5	5	5
Task 4	4	4
Task 3	3	3
Task 2	2	2
Task 1 *(easy)*	1 *(low)*	1 *(low)*

Let's use the chart to understand a sixteen-year-old named David. First, we list tasks that David might attempt, and we rank these tasks from *impossible* to *easy*. We also assess David's ability and his fear of failure, circling the appropriate levels. With his ability level and his fear of failure marked on the chart, we can draw a line that tells us which tasks David will attempt. (See chart on this page.) David's ability is about average, but his fear of failure is high. A high fear of failure is the same as low self-esteem.

Tasks	Ability	Fear of Failure
Task 10 *(impossible)*	10 *(high)*	10 *(high)*
Task 9	9	9
Task 8	8	(8)
Task 7	7	7
Task 6	(6)	6
Task 5	5	5
Task 4	4	4
Task 3	3	3
Task 2	2	2
Task 1 *(easy)*	1 *(low)*	1 *(low)*

The tasks above the line are the tasks that David will not attempt. He will attempt only the easy tasks under the line, and even though people around him consider him successful, he may feel that the tasks could have been done by anyone. As a result, he receives no emotional benefit from having accomplished them. Once in a while, he will get tired of this and, in a rush of enthusiasm and energy, attempt a task that he sees as being impossible. Even if he comes close to being successful in this task, he will make sure that he fails. Then he will say to himself "See, I knew I would fail!" In a perverse way he has managed to successfully predict his own failure. This need to be successful at predicting can be stronger than his need to succeed at the task. As a result his ability level will decline and his fear of failure will increase until his chart looks like this:

Tasks	Ability	Fear of Failure
Task 10 *(impossible)*	10 *(high)*	10 *(high)*
Task 9	9	9
Task 8	8	8
Task 7	7	7
Task 6	6	6
Task 5	5	5
Task 4	4	4
Task 3	3	3
Task 2	2	2
Task 1 *(easy)*	1 *(low)*	1 *(low)*

Now David is immobilized and will probably turn to some type of escape such as drugs, alcohol, sex, or even suicide, to deal with the stresses of life.

The way to change this process is to help David set goals that are within his ability but that are also somewhat challenging. For example, let us say that David's piano teacher has a fairly clear picture of David's ability and has chosen five pieces of music that David could play. When David comes for his lesson, she plays these pieces and asks David to choose the one he wants to learn to play. After making the choice, David and his teacher negotiate a contract. First they decide how long it will take David to learn the piece. David might say something like, "Oh, I can do that in three weeks," or he might say, "That will take me at least two years." What he says will depend on whether he is overly confident or overly discouraged. The teacher may suggest that perhaps six months is a more realistic period. The teacher will also provide clear criteria for judging success. For example, the contract might say:

I, David Jones, will accomplish the following:

1. Learn to play Chopin's prelude by June 4, 1986.

2. Consider myself successful if I can play the piece at a tempo of 90 or above with no more than ten mistakes.

At the end of the agreed-upon period comes the test of David's success. The teacher listens to him play, measures his speed, and counts his mistakes. Instead of saying something vague like, "You did a good job!" the teacher can say: "You played this piece at a tempo of 95 and you made only five mistakes. According to our agreement, you have been successful. Congratulations!" Now David can't say to himself or anyone else, "Well, I really did not do very well."

As a result of having his ability challenged and his success proven, David's ability will begin to increase and his fear of failure will decrease.

Any contract with your children should:

1. Allow them to chose one goal from a limited list of possible goals.

2. Be in writing.

3. Have a clear description of the goal.

4. Specify a time limit.

5. Have a clear definition of success.

Adolescence is one of the most challenging periods of life. Parents and family can do much to create a positive environment for teenagers. Adolescents need to know their strengths are recognized and more highly valued than their weaknesses. Too often adults tend to notice only their children's weaknesses.

Parents also need to be aware of the personalities of their teenagers and to encourage them in their strengths and interests. If a teenager is interested in a certain activity, help him develop his interest. Provide training for him, if possible. Plan family outings with his interests in mind. Help the teenager to display his skills to his friends during activities with them.

Encourage your teenagers to try things that are difficult for them. Expose them to new and challenging activities that they might ordinarily avoid, such as doing service projects or volunteer work, or taking on special tasks in the family. One young man was given the responsibility for the family finances at an early age. At first this was difficult for him and for his parents, but after training and practice he became very capable at managing money. He not only paid the bills on time, but he also became interested in investments and found ways to increase the earning potential of the family.

Parents can help their children by talking about their own successes. By talking positively about themselves and their children, they help their teenagers think in terms of strengths rather than weaknesses. Too often people can identify their weaknesses but not their strengths. When teenagers develop the habit of talking about strengths, they become resilient to discouragement and conflicts that arise in life.

Parents also help their teenagers by being able to bounce back from frustrations, disappointments, and stumbling blocks. Sometimes parents try to present a perfect image to their children, so their children never learn how to deal with problems. Teenagers who see their parents deal with real challenges will be strengthened in their resilience.

Parents should give their children the full and final responsibility for certain tasks or activities around the home. It is one thing to expect that teenagers perform certain tasks, but it is another thing to give them full and final responsibility. When teenagers are given real responsibility, they are more likely to become responsible.

The handing down of beliefs, customs, stories, and activities from parents to children is very important in producing unity in a family. Young children love to talk about their families, and this is encouraged in school and other groups. As a family, you should have activities that give family members a sense of belonging. These can be as simple as making fudge or going skiing. What is important is that they are a part of your life and that they are considered traditions in your family. What you do on holidays, birthdays, and vacations is important, and there should be certain things that children can count on year after year.

Experiences with grandparents, aunts and uncles, and cousins give children a broader understanding of what a family means. One family planned a special evening for grandparents. The children took charge of the meeting, prepared treats, organized a program, and even earned money for small gifts of appreciation. All the children in turn told of their feelings of appreciation for their grandparents.

Your children will remember the fun times you have had together as a family more than anything else. Children who come from homes where there has been a lot of fun and activity learn that life can be fun and rewarding. Plan one day each week or every other week just for family fun. Show by your example that this comes first, before social or business obligations.

Parents generally tend to underestimate their children. Children thrive and family spirit soars when expectations are high and much responsibility is given. Parents who don't allow their youngsters the experiences of working, sharing, and giving — even the most affluent of parents — are rearing deprived children.

A family that has a strong moral fiber is more able to stand the buffetings of the world and come out whole. Expressions of love and warmth are as vital to the family as sunshine and rain to the natural world. Children learn from experience. If they live in a home where they have positive emotional and moral experiences, their feelings of self-worth are greatly enhanced and they are able to give more freely of themselves in other relationships. Do not take it for granted that your children know what you believe in. Parents need to share their ideas and beliefs rather than preach them. Your real preaching comes in how well your behavior reflects what you say you believe in.

As you think about what is happening in your family don't dwell on the problems you see. Spend time becoming aware of and talking about the strengths and resources within your family. You will, of course, see problems. But don't try to solve all your problems at once. Instead, pick a place to start and attempt to make some changes in only one area that has a good likelihood of success. Allow yourself to make mistakes as you work on your problems. The only real mistake that you cannot recover from is the failure to try.

4

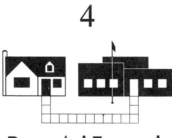

Parental Example

I am often asked by parents to counsel with their children about various difficulties in school. I usually say I want to talk to the parents first. Many parents understand the need for this, but some say: "But I don't have a problem — my son does."

While talking to the parents, I usually ask a few specific questions:

1. How much time do you spend reading significant books?

2. When was the last time you shared a significant learning experience with your family?

3. Do your children often see you learning a new concept or new behavior?

4. How much control do you have over your own watching of television?

I have found the answers to these questions to be significant predictors of how well the parents help their children succeed at school.

To begin with, parents need to realize that reading is a key element in success at school. Children will not learn to enjoy reading unless parents provide an atmosphere to encourage it. Are there books in the home? Are books and reading an important part of the parents' activities? Are the children given books at an early age? Do the parents read to their children? It is unrealistic and even unfair to expect that children will suddenly enjoy reading when they enter school if no groundwork has been laid for them.

Parents can do much to help their children gain an appreciation for reading. You may not need to worry so much about the skill of reading as about helping your children learn that reading is enjoyable. With preschool children, you can do the following things:

1. Talk to your child. Answer your children's questions, and name things in your home and things that you see as you drive or walk outside. Being able to use words will help your children to understand what they read in the future.

2. Listen to your children. Take time to encourage them to talk about what they do and how they feel.

3. Read to your children every day. Take time to read rhymes, poems, or stories and then talk about them. Help your children realize that reading is fun. Young children enjoy picture books and understand what is on the pages by talking about the pictures. After several readings, your children may be able to say some of the words with you, or you can pause and wait for them to continue with the next word. Encourage the children to start to pick out words or letters on a page, but don't push them.

4. Go places with your children. Take short trips to town, the library, a zoo, a circus, or a park and talk about what you see and about signs or words that you see. Background knowledge from actually doing and seeing many things will help children understand what they read. Browse through a simple encyclopedia to look at pictures and read short descriptions of a wide variety of things in the world.

5. Play games to help your children learn numbers, colors, and words. Count objects. Ask, "What is red in this room?" "Is the dog under the table, beside the table, or on top of the table?"

Families need to provide time for members of the family to share what they have been reading and learning. Some families make dinnertime a time for family discussion. They can do this only if they are learning something worth talking about. In some cases parents can talk repeatedly about the things they have talked about many times before, and their children soon learn to quit listening. They get tired, and who can blame them?

How parents talk about school also affects how their children feel about school. From an early age, children sometimes expect to have negative experiences in school because of what they have heard from their parents. Many people have had negative experiences in school, but we tend to remember and talk about our negative experiences and forget or fail to mention our positive ones. Children need to understand that while all is not perfect in school, many teachers and administrators are sincerely interested in helping them learn and grow. If they do meet school personnel who really are unkind or even incompetent, you can deal with those situations as they occur.

It is important that children feel that their parents are willing to help them with school assignments. Do help your children, but don't become so involved that you take over the assignment. You may find some of the assignments are not familiar to you or that methods and materials are presented that you do not understand. You might have to do some research on your own or request some help from the teacher or the PTA.

As you get involved in homework assignments or actually do some remedial tutoring, remember that your goal is to make your involvement with your children a pleasant experience. Give them lots of encouragement and make your approach challenging and helpful rather than threatening. You will get more mileage out of several short work periods than you will out of one or two long ones. You might even find an interesting educational game that will help your children master the skills or concepts involved.

Try to teach your children that they are responsible for their own learning. They may have teachers who are ineffective, but that only means that they have to work harder. No one can learn something for someone else. That is one reason why you should talk with your children's teachers occasionally. You need to have an accurate picture of your children's progress and be aware of any problems or difficulties they are having.

There are thousands of simple activities you can do with your children to help them learn basic learning skills. Here are a few possibilities:

1. *Analyze a story together.* After a story has been read, ask questions about the main characters, the minor characters, and their relationships. Describe the main plot.

2. *Read homework aloud.* Have a student read papers aloud before turning them in to the teacher. Do they say what was intended? Parents can read a paper to a child exactly at it was written, not pausing unless the punctuation so indicates. Then the student can see if the paper says what it was meant to.

3. *Play "Robot".* Follow exactly the instructions a child gives you in performing some activity. The child must break the activity into its parts and put them in the right sequence to be an effective master of the robot.

The list can go on and on. Find a Parent Education Resource Center in your area or school district and ask for other simple learning activities you can do at home.

Children are faced with a multitude of influences that are not always positive. Many of these influences are right in their own home. Many parents complain about what their children are learning from television, but these same parents seem to do little to control this important influence in their home. Parents cannot expect to control their children's television watching unless they first get control over their own. Some families plan together what to watch each week. They have a rule that no member of the family can turn on the television just to see what is on. If you try this, be sure to stick to your plan. You may include several times for certain members of the family to watch television for relaxation or enjoyment, but generally you should try to schedule programs that are educational in some way. You may even want to record those programs that you think are worth watching so that you can set your own times to watch them.

Sometimes the way you watch television is just as important as what you watch. If a family sits in stony silence watching television, the children have a tendency to absorb the values and life-styles that are portrayed and perhaps even try to emulate them. This, of course, is not always positive. Parents may try to deal with this by making comments such as "Oh! That is so awful!" or "I really don't like you watching that!" Instead of doing this, try to start a dialogue about what is happening. Ask such questions as "What do you think is really happening there?" "How would you feel if you were that person?" "How might that situation be like events that you have experienced?" "What would be a better way of dealing with that situation?" "Would you be likely to do something like that?"

Most children have had the experience of being very excited about something advertised on television. But they soon learn that what is portrayed on television is not usually exactly what they end up with. Many have even learned to become quite adept at picking out advertising that is less than accurate or realistic. You need to help them to see that much the same thing can occur in television programs. You might say something like this: "Do you remember when you saw —— advertised and you wanted me to buy it for you? You were not very happy with that when you actually got it because it did not live up to your expectations. Well, many television programs are like that. They may not be selling a product, but they may be selling a certain life-style or value system. As you watch the program, you begin to identify with that life-style, and it may be years later that you discover that you have bought a rotten apple. So when you watch television programs, you need to watch them more critically so that what they are presenting does not begin to affect the way you develop as a person."

As you teach your children to be more aware of the influences that outside factors have on them, they will become better able to make wise choices. You, too, should learn to make wise choices about what effect outside forces have on your children. Many of these influences merely fill voids that have not been filled by careful planning on the part of parents. For example, parents often complain about the music their children listen to, but they have only themselves to blame. Many of today's lyrics are negative. But children will be attracted to music of some kind — that you can count on. You can begin introducing your children at an early age to good music and make music a fun part of your family life. Find music teachers who are interested in helping your children enjoy music before they push them into the rigors of technical training. Some families have made it a rule that each child learn to play a musical instrument of some kind. It is wise to let your children help decide what instrument they want to play, but once they have decided, music lessons should probably be mandatory until age sixteen.

Parents need to learn about music. Your home should have a collection of good music, and you should sometimes listen to music instead of watching television. There is much classical music that children and adults can enjoy together without any musical training. There is, however, much more good music that takes some training to be able to enjoy. Support good music programs in the schools and see to it that these programs are not short-changed in the budget battle. In the long run, this training could be what keeps your child from getting into trouble during the teenage years.

Encourage your children to get involved in some kind of extracurricular activity at school. Often the social skills that can be learned in this way are every bit as important as anything that will be learned in class. These activities will help your children build on their interests and their self-esteem. Students who merely go to school and return home are missing a great opportunity to learn and grow. Many students will not become involved in activities at school without encouragement from parents. Sit down with your children and explore the possibilities. You might have to visit the school to get a list of the organizations, clubs, and activities.

Children need to feel that they are successful and that they are making progress. One of the main jobs of parents is to control their children's environment so that they will feel this way.

I am constantly amazed at how little conversation takes place between children and parents. Families need to talk so that parents can share positive values and ideas with their children on a wide variety of topics.

One topic parents should discuss with their children is sex. The loving, accepting, and understanding family environment provides the best setting to teach children about reproduction. This allows children to learn with a minimum of apprehension, confusion, and anxiety. Children are not born knowing about sex, but all children, in some way and at their own speed, do learn about it. Parents are in the best position to be sensitive to the individual needs and readiness of each of their children.

It is not perhaps even so important that parents discuss the biological "facts of life" with their children as it is that they discuss the values and attitudes about sex and sexuality that they think are important. Parents need to indicate a willingness to discuss this issue and be available to answer questions. In order for this to be effective, parents need to talk first to each other about what they think is important and about what role they think sex should play in a person's life. Children want to hear positive ideas and values from their parents rather than just a series of biological facts and warnings of things to avoid.

Many teenagers become involved in a variety of sexual behaviors because they are trying to find the human warmth and closeness that they seem to be missing in their lives. They do not really realize that the warmth, closeness, and understanding they are seeking has nothing to do with sex or even with sexuality. It has to do with establishing close human relationships. Without such a relationship, sex can be shallow and meaningless. Children are not likely to learn these important concepts at school. Parents need to begin early to help their children understand these things.

Parents need to realize that they can set the tone for how their children feel about a wide variety of issues. You cannot be held responsible for all that goes on in the lives of your children in regard to school. But many parents set their children up to fail by what they do and say. Even with your very best efforts, your children may have problems that you cannot deal with effectively without getting help from someone outside the family. But try to make sure that you are not helping to create problems for your children before they even get to the school doors.

Try evaluating the learning climate in your home by answering the following questions. After you have written down your answers, read the discussion that follows.

Family Communication
1. T F Members of our family help and support one another.
2. T F We say anything we want to as long as the language is appropriate.
3. T F We tell each other about our personal problems.
4. T F Financial matters are openly discussed in our family.
5. T F We are usually careful about what we say to each other.
6. T F We have many spontaneous discussions in our family.
7. T F We are not really encouraged to speak up for ourselves in our family.
8. T F We rarely have intellectual discussions.

Productivity
1. T F Activities in our family are fairly carefully planned.
2. T F Each person's responsibilities are clearly defined in our family.
3. T F "Work before play" is the rule in our family.
4. T F Dishes are usually done immediately after eating.
5. T F Being on time is important in our family.
6. T F We put a lot of energy into what we do at home.
7. T F We are generally neat and orderly.
8. T F Getting ahead in life is important in our family.
9. T F In our family, each person is strongly encouraged to be independent.

Nurturance and Affection
1. T F Family members are rarely ordered around.
2. T F Family members often criticize each other.
3. T F Someone usually gets upset if anyone complains in our family.
4. T F Family members sometimes hit each other.
5. T F If there is a disagreement in our family, we try hard to smooth things over and keep the peace at all costs.
6. T F Family members often try to out-do each other.
7. T F Family members are often compared with others as to how well they are doing at work or school.
8. T F Family members hardly ever lose their tempers.
9. T F There is little group spirit in our family.
10. T F We get along well with each other.
11. T F There is plenty of time and attention for everyone in our family.

Stable Family Organization
1. T F Our family has a few clear rules to follow.
2. T F We are generally neat and orderly.
3. T F We come and go as we want to.
4. T F We have set ways of doing things at home.
5. T F We emphasize following the rules.
6. T F People change their minds often.
7. T F Everyone has an equal contribution to make in family decisions.
8. T F We can do whatever we want to.
9. T F Rules are flexible in our household.

Achievement by Example
1. T F We frequently read to our children and we ourselves read where our children can see us.
2. T F We often tell about successes we have had in school.
3. T F When family members accomplish something, they are recognized and praised.

4. T F We are often able to help children with their school assignments.

5. T F We seldom say that we are dumb or that we failed in school.

6. T F We openly communicate that we expect our children to do well in school without pressuring them too much.

7. T F We describe school as a fun place where our children can learn and grow.

8. T F We tell our children that teachers are genuinely concerned about them and want to help them.

Family Communication. Score 1 point for each correct answer: 1-T, 2-T, 3-T, 4-T, 5-F, 6-T, 7-F, 8-F.

Each family has its own style of communicating. This includes the kinds of things talked about and how much people talk to each other. When family members communicate often, they learn to absorb larger amounts of information. This helps children learn more easily at school. If your conversations are brief, your children may have problems paying attention to teachers for more than a few minutes. The more verbal communication there is in the home, the easier it is for children to succeed in the verbal world of school. It is also important that you spend time listening to your children. This will help them learn how to express their thoughts and feelings.

Productivity. Score 1 point for each true statement.

Families have different styles of accomplishing things. There are four characteristics of productivity that relate closely to achievement in school:

1. *Independent work.* Children benefit when they have some of their own tasks to perform by a certain time. They learn to do things on their own and to be responsible. This helps them greatly with homework and other independent projects.

2. *Cooperative work*. School requires that children work together. Cooperation is best taught in the home. It is very difficult for children to learn to work well with others in school if cooperation is not taught and encouraged at home.

3. *Task completion*. Families can teach children to persevere until the work is completed. The lack of this skill is probably the greatest cause of failure in school.

4. *Pride in achieving*. Self-esteem is partly determined by feelings of accomplishment. Parents need to make sure that their children experience success regularly. Children benefit when they know parents approve of their abilities. If parents are too harsh and critical, their children may become afraid of failure and refrain from attempting anything.

Nurturance and Affection. Score 1 point for 1-T, 2-F, 3-F, 4-5, 5-T, 6-F, 7-F, 8-T, 9-F, 10-T, 11-T.

The emotional stability of children depends on their belief that people will like them and approve of them. When families are loving and openly nurturing, children will transfer that experience to other situations with school and friends. When children are frightened of disapproval, it is difficult for them to concentrate, perform, and succeed. Avoid using competition to motivate children at home. If your children are competitive, stress the importance of enjoying participation in sports without becoming overly concerned about winning or losing. Also, put pressure on your school to control destructive competition.

Stable Family Organization. Score 1 point for 1-F, 2-T, 3-F, 4-T, 5- T, 6-F, 7-T, 8-F, 9-F.

There is clear evidence that successful children come from families where rules and routines are a part of the family life. Parents in these families are able to set up positive routines for such events as meals, getting up in the morning, going to bed, family trips, and so on.

Achievement by Example. Score 1 point for each true statement.

Children form attitudes about achieving and learning based on the example parents set. That is, parents who have had negative school experiences while they were young and dwell on those experiences tend to transmit negative attitudes to their children, who are often led to expect the same types of experiences. If parents do not show that they feel that learning and school are important by their behavior and their conversations, then children are not likely to feel education is very important.

Parents can do much to support their children's efforts to succeed in school. Parents first need to look at their own behavior, attitudes, and feelings and make any needed changes. Then they can turn their attention to changing things in the family.

5

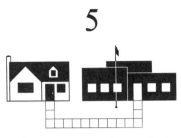

Working with School and Community

No matter how effective parents are they cannot hope to be as successful with their children as they would like to be because of the many other influences upon them. For that reason, parents must find ways to become involved in the school and the community.

The relationships that parents and teachers are able to establish with youth are far more important during the teenage years than any academic program. The home enivronment needs to be characterized by a clear and consistent structure, open communication, and unconditional positive regard (good old-fashioned love). If parents are united and listen to each other and to their children without criticism or evaluation, they and their children can come to agree upon the significant values accepted in the family. From this agreement comes the strength to succeed in life and to avoid some of the pitfalls of growing up.

The relationships that teenagers develop with adults outside the family are important in furthering the progress begun in the home. We need teachers, counselors, and youth leaders with the ability and willingness to build close relationships with youth. Adults can learn these skills, but people with certain personalities are easier to train than others, so proper selection of those who are going to work with our youth is important.

Teenagers need to feel independent from their parents, but at the same time, they need some confirmation of the values and ideas they have received from their parents. If teenagers have no meaningful relationships with adults outside their family, they will turn to their peers for what they need. In most instances, teachers can no longer fill this role because of large class sizes. But we can encourage our children to become involved in extracurricular activities that will provide them with the opportunity to interact with other adults.

Young people have a strong need to feel accepted. What most adults do not realize is that this need can best be filled by adults outside the family who are willing to work with the parents. If teenagers feel accepted and valued by adults (parents, teachers, youth workers, principals, counselors), they will feel accepted by other young people.

What happens to our teenagers is more affected by adults than we realize. What seems to be happening at present is that too many adults have failed to be what our youth need them to be. It is because of this failure that peer-group pressure has become such a powerful negative force. We must make an effort to help adults to do a better job in the home, in the church, at school, and in the community.

When it comes right down to it, the parents own the schools. Far too often, parents do not remember whom they voted for in the last school-board election, and when they do remember, they do not know what position that person has taken on important educational issues. School-board meetings may be boring to many, but parents need to know what occurs in them and what decisions are made. Often decisions are made there on some personal whim of an administrator or under pressure from a small vocal minority. Perhaps not all parents can attend all board meetings, but organizations like the PTA or other neighborhood organizations could help to arrange a schedule so that parents could take turns attending and reporting back to their neighborhood group. This way the feelings of a larger number of parents can be represented at these important meetings.

PTSA (Parent Teacher Student Association) groups at the local school level are vital to having an effective school system that meets the needs of each child. One local PTA group accepted the challenge to have a trained parent in every classroom at every hour. At first their project was met with resistance from teachers and parents. The PTA leaders took great care to interview all the teachers and found out what the teachers wanted done for them in the classroom. Parents were then trained to do only the things that teachers had indicated would be helpful. This association has led to a positive climate in the school and positive interactions between parents, teachers, administrators, and students.

One of the projects that came out of this arrangement was a weekly newsletter published by the parent volunteers. The newsletter told about what had happened in the classrooms during the past week and what would be going on in the classrooms during the next week. It gave three or four learning activities that parents could do at home with their children to prepare them for the coming week's activities. These parents and teachers became a team working to help the children reach their potential.

Another PTA group interviewed all of the teachers during the summer. Then in the fall, they distributed a calendar of events in each classroom to the parents. This meant that the teachers had to have an outline of their whole year's curriculum. The calendar listed the weekly topic in each class and suggested related learning activities parents could provide for their children.

Parents often feel that by attending back-to-school night and paying their PTA dues, they have done their duty; but this is not enough. Parents must help convince government leaders and other parents that education is our highest priority. Many of the difficulties students face come from the fact that too many classrooms are overcrowded. Teachers may be able to teach certain material effectively in classes with thirty to forty students, but to teach in a way that will raise students' self-esteem, we need classes of twenty to thirty students. Only parents can convince the public and government leaders to provide for the funding that would be needed.

Parents should be actively concerned about the education of their children, but this concern should not present an added burden. It should mean a new style of living and learning with children and being in the community. Parents teach incidentally as a natural outgrowth of daily interaction with their children. Part of the responsibility shared by parents is to find ways to identify and attract the best qualified people into the teaching field and to make sure that they are properly trained and rewarded for their service.

Parents need to provide more support and background for their children as well as to build a more positive relationship with their schools. In the past, some parents have fought to get the schools to provide special assistance and support for their children's special needs. Recently, however, many of these parents have discovered that their children are more like other children than they are different from them. We have learned that we must all work together to develop and maintain a supportive atmosphere at school so the individual needs of all students are satisfied.

We can accomplish many things by working together in groups that no one person would be able to accomplish alone. Some of the things parents could do to help children with exceptional needs, improve the quality of family life, and develop better relationships between parents and schools include the following:

1. Identify existing resources and programs that might already fill certain needs.

2. Develop parent training and support groups with correlation of special needs through local PTA officers. State PTA organizations can help local PTA groups become aware of individual needs of students and parents.

3. Help develop resource centers where parents can get answers to their questions about how to help their children.

4. Emphasize the Student Education Plan. Under this plan, teachers, parents, and students meet together to develop a specialized and specific educational program for each child. Specific goals and ways to evaluate the accomplishment of these goals are established in writing. The PTA organization might conduct "critical issues" conferences or workshops with students during the day while the teachers meet individually with each student to develop individualized plans. Parents should also be involved in this program.

5. Develop surrogate parent programs for children who need them and find ways to develop awareness of children's hidden handicaps and special needs.

6. Give equal treatment to all exceptional children instead of dealing with separate and fragmented groups.

7. Provide resource specialists where needed with the PTA acting as a source of communication and coordination.

8. Help local PTA units hold parent training workshops (at least three a year). These workshops would be a family affair. Parents would be involved in training while younger children would enjoy story-telling, entertainment, or a nursery.

9. Encourage PTA groups and community education programs to work together to provide parent-training courses with possible college credit. These courses could deal with parenting skills as well as skills needed to help children with homework.

10. Encourage schools to provide a parent resource area in their media centers.

11. Develop educational television programs for parents— perhaps live question-and-answer call-in programs with panels of experts.

12. Encourage elementary PTA groups to help parents of preschool children prepare their children to succeed in school. They could provide information to help parents choose effective day-care programs and to orient students entering school for the first time.

13. Distribute information on how parents can be involved in learning activities at home.

14. Make school personnel aware of family and parent needs.

15. Encourage other parents to be involved in the school system.

16. Develop more effective resources for "latchkey" children.

17. Develop support groups and special resources to help single parents deal with their unique problems.

18. Develop the PTA as the coordinator of educational programs and conferences.

19. Help schools develop incentives for parents to become involved with their children's education.

20. Have the PTA develop media articles and programs on the advantages of better communication among parents, administrators and teachers.

21. Find better ways to hold parent-teacher conferences, perhaps involving students.

22. Become involved in curriculum decisions.

23. Help train new PTA officers (perhaps through community education courses) on how to work with the schools.

24. Have PTA units organize and coordinate regular school newsletters to help parents understand what they can do to help teachers and children.

25. Help PTA groups reach parents who have not been involved before through using persistent effort; showing parents how to be involved in school decisions; encouraging teachers to visit homes to invite parents to be involved; asking parent volunteers to visit homes; involving a variety of people, including those with complaints; developing small neighborhood discussion groups; and involving more fathers — perhaps by encouraging employers to give employees incentives for taking time to work with the PTA.

26. Find ways to overcome the problems that block parental involvement: feeling intimidated or out of place; not having enough time; not knowing how to get involved.

27. Encourage children to help their parents become involved.

28. Realize that the principal is the key to the climate that exists in the school. Help train the principal to deal with this important area.

29. Work with educators to change the rules and structures that get in the way of effective education. This would include completely eliminating the use of the normal curve for assigning grades. In it's place teachers should develop an effective criterion-based grading system.

30. Insist that grades be based on tests of academic performance or progress with some element allowed for partici-

pation. Ask teachers to eliminate automatic academic failure for a certain number of absences. Additional grades for citizenship or attendance can be given to indicate the student's total performance.

31. Get parents and teachers more involved in making decisions. Too many decisions about our schools are made by administrators, executives, or lobbyists who know nothing about what the real possibilities are.

Every time we study the problems facing our youth, we discover two basic ideas. First, children are not learning the basic skills at home that they need to have. Second, the schools are not as positive and effective as they need to be.

These two elements are clearly evident in studies on drug and alcohol abuse, teenage suicide, and teenage pregnancy. Therefore we must deal with these two problems. We can help provide training for parents to give the skills they need to be effective with their children, but we cannot require them to accept this training, nor can we select those who ought to be parents. We can, however, require effective training of our school personnel, and we can even select those teachers who are most capable of benefiting from this training and putting it into practice.

We have failed to train teachers to deal with the problems of developing human beings. We have worked so hard to develop scientists and mathematicians in our push for "excellence in education" that we have not developed capable human beings.

In light of this situation, parents need to work for changes in the process of selecting and training teachers, counselors, and administrators using these guidelines:

Teachers. Teachers need to be selected more carefully on the basis of their personality and basic skills in dealing with people. Tests are available and could be developed that would help us to determine these characteristics. Prospective teachers need to be introduced into the classroom setting earlier than at present. At least forty hours of classroom experience should be required before the end of their junior year in college. They should also be required to take practical and experience-based courses that would help them to deal with the pressures and problems they will face in dealing with today's teenagers. This is every bit as important as preparing in their academic area. They must know as much if not more about *how* to teach teenagers than they know about *what* to teach. This would require that those who teach courses in a college of education do a much better job of presenting an example of effective teaching than they have in the past.

Once certified, teachers need to be rewarded financially and in many other ways for their performance. Parents need to take some responsibility for making teachers feel respected and appreciated for the work they do. There is perhaps no other more important task in our society than educating our youth, and we need to make sure that all members of our society recognize that fact.

Counselors. School counselors are not usually trained to deal with the emotional and psychological needs of youth. Those who are capable of assisting young people with emotional problems are usually prevented from doing so by their clerical and administrative duties. Counselors should be required to receive much more training in adolescent psychology and counseling theory and practice. They should perhaps *not* be required to have a teaching certificate. There are qualified people who could be trained to be effective school counselors who have not had a teaching background. Many teachers become counselors because they have not been successful in the classroom. A student at a major high school, when asked if she would go to any of the counselors at her school, replied, "Oh, no! They are all more interested in doing paperwork than they are in talking to students." Once in the schools, counselors who are trained to work with youth should be allowed to do so, and clerks should be hired to do the paperwork.

Administrators. Administrators particularly should be selected on their ability to build positive relationships with students, teachers, and parents. The last thing we need is people who have decided to become principals because they failed as teachers. The key to developing an emotional climate for growth is the principal. Principals should be selected for administrative training very carefully. That training should include training in organizational behavior and how to create positive growth environments—not how to become a rigid bureaucrat. Once trained and functioning as administrators, principals should be *required* to teach at least one course so that they keep their contact with students and lighten the load of other teachers.

We must do something to improve our children's education or we are going to continue to lose more and more of them to drugs, alcohol, sex, or suicide. We must create environments where they can feel successful in coping with the problems of life. If we do not significantly change things, I cannot help but feel that we will see present problems grow to epidemic proportions. Appropriate selection of teachers, counselors, and administrators is probably more important than any aspect of training or even any aspects of how schools are organized.

We do not need to spend time finding fault or deciding where the blame lies. We need to work together to find creative, constructive solutions. Educators need to be educators and not bureaucrats. Educators need to realize that they need help from parents, and they should invite and reward parent participation in making decisions and in the day-to-day operations of the school. Parents need to take their responsibility seriously and become involved in their children's education. Community organizations need to become involved. Together, we can find ways to improve the environment, at home and at school so that our children can succeed in school and in life. It depends on us.

Index